Audit Committee Formation in the Aftermath of the 2007–2009 Global Financial Crisis, Volume II

Audit Committee Formation in the Aftermath of the 2007–2009 Global Financial Crisis, Volume II

Responsibilities and Sustainability

Zabihollah Rezaee

BEP BUSINESS EXPERT PRESS

Audit Committee Formation in the Aftermath of the 2007–2009 Global Financial Crisis, Volume II: Responsibilities and Sustainability

First published in 2016 by
Business Expert Press, LLC
222 East 46th Street, New York, NY 10017
www.businessexpertpress.com

ISBN-13: 978-1-63157-154-1 (paperback)
ISBN-13: 978-1-63157-155-8 (e-book)

Business Expert Press Financial Accounting and Auditing Collection

Collection ISSN: 2151-2795 (print)
Collection ISSN: 2151-2817 (electronic)

Cover and interior design by S4Carlisle Publishing Services
Private Ltd., Chennai, India

First edition: 2016

10 9 8 7 6 5 4 3 2 1

Printed in the United States of America

Abstract

The audit committee, as an integral component of corporate governance, has gained considerable attention in the aftermath of 2007–2009 global financial crisis. The audit committee's role has evolved from a voluntary liaison between management and external auditors to the standing committee of the board of directors in overseeing all aspects of corporate governance, financial reporting, internal controls, risk assessment, and audit activities. This book addresses the determinants of audit committee oversight effectiveness, including their composition, independence, authority, resources, diligence, and activities. Today, audit committees operate in an environment of ever-increasing corporate governance reforms established to protect investors and the public from receiving misleading financial statements and related audit reports. Audit committees, in complying with emerging corporate governance reforms, are striving to improve their oversight effectiveness to discharge their oversight responsibilities.

This book is organized into three separate volumes, and each volume can be utilized separately or in an integrated form. The first volume addresses the formation of the audit committee, its relevance, sources, structure and roles; the second volume focuses on the oversight functions of the audit committee; and the third volume presents the emerging issues of audit committees. The first volume consists of five chapters that examine the relevance and fundamentals of the audit committees as well as the determinants of audit committee effectiveness. The second volume consists of nine chapters on financial, auditing, internal control, risk management, ethics and compliance, antifraud, and other oversight functions of the audit committee. The third volume consists of several chapters on the emerging issues of audit committees pertaining to evaluation, education, reporting, and accountability as well as audit committees of private companies, governmental entities, and not-for-profit organizations.

The three volumes of this book present the essential and fundamental aspects and functions of audit committees, with a keen focus on their working relationship with other corporate governance participants including the board of directors, executives, internal auditors, external auditors, legal counsel, financial analysts, investment bankers, governing bodies, standard setters, and other stakeholders. Anyone who is involved with corporate governance, the financial reporting process, and audit functions should be interested in this book. Specifically, corporations and their executives, the boards of directors and audit committees, internal and external auditors, accountants, governing bodies, users of financial statements (investors, creditors, pensioners), business schools, and other professionals (attorneys, financial analysts, bankers) will benefit from this book. The three volumes of the book focus on up-to-date corporate governance measures and best practices in the aftermath of the global financial crisis and their impacts on audit committee effectiveness.

Keywords

Audit Committee, Corporate Governance, Oversight Effectiveness, Financial Reports, Audit Functions, Risk Assessment, Internal Controls, Business Ethics, Audit Committee Structure, Composition, Responsibilities and Accountability

Contents

Acknowledgments

I acknowledge the Securities and Exchange Commission, the Public Company Accounting Oversight Board, the American Institute of Certified Public Accountants, and Big Four Accounting Firms for permission to quote and reference their professional standards and other publications.

The encouragement and support of my colleagues at the University of Memphis are also acknowledged. Specifically, two of my graduate assistants, Mr. Rob Palmer and Mr. Josh McDonald provided invaluable assistance. I thank the members of the Business Expert Press team and S4Carlisle Publishing Services for their hard work and dedication in editing the book, including Stewart Mattson, Scott Isenberg, Scott Showalter and Jan Williams, Mark Bettner, Michael Coyne, and Premkumar Narayanan.

My sincere thanks are due to my family, my wife Soheila, and my children Rose and Nick. Without their love, enthusiasm, and support, this book would not have come to fruition when it did.

Zabihollah Rezaee
May 12, 2016

Introduction

To effectively fulfill their new challenging oversight functions and responsibilities in the aftermath of the global 2007–2009 financial crisis, audit committees are seeking guidance and best practices. This volume is intended to provide such guidance and best practices regarding oversight functions of the audit committee in the areas of corporate governance, financial reporting, internal controls, and audit activities. The ever-changing corporate governance and the financial reporting process continue to present audit committees with challenges and opportunities to improve the effectiveness of their oversight function. Recent regulatory reforms have shifted some of management's financial reporting and audit involvement responsibilities to the audit committee. New regulatory reforms and best practices have conferred upon audit committee's certain duties that were previously the domain of management (e.g., hiring and firing external auditors, overseeing internal audit functions, setting audit fees).

To be able to effectively perform the above oversight functions and discharge their responsibilities to investors, audit committees must understand what information they need, how to analyze it and what questions to ask to gain insights and make informed decisions. Thus, best practices of audit committees will continue to be in the following areas:

1. Governance and strategic oversight
2. Risk oversight and risk management
3. Committee composition, independence, effectiveness, and dynamics
4. Oversight of financial reporting
5. Oversight of internal controls
6. Oversight of compliance, ethics, and whistle-blowing programs
7. Oversight of IT technologies and their challenges, opportunities, and threats
8. Relationship with independent auditor and oversight of audit activities
9. Interaction with management and review of operational, reporting, governance, and compliance activities

The oversight function of corporate governance is assumed by the entire board of directors as representative of shareholders and is typically delegated by the board of directors to various board committees. However, the entire board remains responsible for the oversight of these delegated functions. The eight chapters presented in this volume examine the major oversight functions of audit committees. Chapter 1 discusses the corporate governance oversight function of audit committees in overseeing strategic managerial decisions. Chapter 2 presents the financial reporting oversight functions of audit committees in overseeing the quality, quantity, integrity, reliability, credibility, and transparency of financial reports. Chapter 3 examines the external auditing oversight function of audit committees in overseeing the objectivity, credibility, and effectiveness of audit and permissible non-audit services provided by external auditors. Chapter 4 discusses the internal audit oversight function of audit committees in overseeing the effectiveness of both the design and operation of internal controls in general and internal control over financial reporting in particular. Chapter 5 examines the risk oversight function of audit committees in general and the enterprise risk management (ERM) in particular. Chapter 6 describes the fraud risk assessment oversight function of audit committees in overseeing antifraud programs designed to prevent, detect, and correct occupational fraud including financial statement fraud, money laundering, and corruptions. Chapter 7 presents the ethics and compliance oversight function of the audit committee in overseeing the establishment, implementation, and compliance with a corporate code of ethics. Chapter 8 discusses the tax consideration oversight function and the whistle-blower oversight function of audit committees in overseeing procedures designed to facilitate the whistle-blowing process and to protect whistle-blowers.

CHAPTER 1:   CORPORATE GOVERNANCE OVERSIGHT
             FUNCTION OF THE AUDIT COMMITTEE
CHAPTER 2:   FINANCIAL REPORTING OVERSIGHT
             FUNCTION OF THE AUDIT COMMITTEE
CHAPTER 3:   EXTERNAL AUDITOR OVERSIGHT
             FUNCTION OF THE AUDIT COMMITTEE

Corporate Governance Oversight Function of the Audit Committee

Executive Summary

As the standing committee of the board of directors, the audit committee is an integral component of corporate governance. The corporate governance oversight of the audit committee is defined in its charter in participating with others in charge of governance in ensuring corporate governance effectiveness. Recent corporate governance reforms require that the audit committee interact with the board of directors, management, internal auditors, external auditors, legal counsel, financial advisors, regulators, and investors as discussed in this chapter.

Introduction

The analysis of the reported financial scandals of the late 1990s and the early 2000s as well as the 2007–2009 global financial crises points to a consistent pattern of lapses in the audit committee oversight function. This raises the question: Where was the audit committee? Audit committees should function to protect investors' interests' by taking the lead on oversight responsibilities in the areas of financial reporting, internal controls, risk assessment, audit activities, and compliance with applicable laws, and regulations. Recent corporate governance reforms have provided new challenges and opportunities for audit committees. To address these challenges and opportunities effectively, audit committees are seeking an appropriate balance between advising management and overseeing its performance in the areas of financial reporting; internal controls; risk management; audit functions; legal compliance; and the establishment of a whistle-blowing program and codes of business conducts.

Corporate Governance Oversight Function

The company's board of directors as the representative of shareholders has the ultimate fiduciary responsibility for safeguarding and advancing the interests of shareholders and thus creating shareholder value. As one of the three mandatory standing board committees (audit, compensation, and nominating committees) and in representing the board of directors, the audit committee often participates in establishing corporate goals and policies and reviewing management's execution of those policies in achieving the company's goals. The entire board of directors, including the audit committee, usually assesses the company's strategic decisions and actions in creating and enhancing sustainable shareholder value while protecting the interests of other stakeholders including creditors, suppliers, customers, employees, society, and the environment). An effective audit committee should understand the company's corporate governance structure, including the business, economic, social, and political environment performance. Representing shareholders, the audit committee should understand the company's major operating, investing, and financing activities while taking care not to usurp managerial prerogatives. The audit committee should oversee management's operating, financing, and investment activities by reviewing significant and potential opportunities and challenges facing the company in pursuit of the creation of shareholder value.

Financial reporting information risks are usually affected by business risks that are associated with the company's business problems. Thus, the audit committee should review the company's major contracts, investments, and expenditures for various divisions and plants, which might cause problems and analyze management's responses to those challenges. Recent corporate governance reforms (Sarbanes–Oxley Act of 2002 [SOX][1], Dodd–Frank Act [DOF][2], Securities and Exchange Commission [SEC][3] implementation rules) have created more oversight responsibilities for audit committees and their involvements in corporate governance activities, including accepting more fiduciary and accountability responsibilities.

The audit committee is considered an integral component of the company's corporate governance, and, as such, the audit committee interacts with other corporate governance participants including management, the internal auditor, the external auditor, legal counsel, users, and standard-setting bodies. The remainder of this chapter explores the audit committee's interactions with others typically involved in a company's corporate governance oversight function.

Audit Committee Interactions with the Board of Directors

The board of directors bears full responsibility for the company's decisions, actions, and affairs. An audit committee represents the board of directors in that the former serves as a standing committee of the latter. The establishment of the audit committee as the standing committee of the board is based on the premise of the need for specialization within the board of directors. The board of directors is ultimately accountable to investors for the company's performance, affairs, business, and financial reports. Thus, the audit committee, on behalf of the board of directors, represents investors and is accountable for protecting their interests. In this respect, an audit committee represents both the board of directors and the shareholders. The audit committee assists the board of directors in fulfilling its responsibilities by bringing specialization and expertise to the board in the areas of financial reporting, internal controls, and audit activities. The board of directors typically appoints members of the board to the audit committee, thereby reinforcing the committee's ultimate responsibility to the board of directors.

Effective compliance with new corporate governance reforms, complexity of business, globalization, and technological advances have encouraged the board of directors to more effectively utilize the expertise, knowledge, and efforts of its audit committee. Boards of directors are ultimately responsible for overseeing firms' strategic decisions, financial reporting procedures, internal control systems, risk assessment activities, audit practices, and corporate governance systems to protect interests of shareholders. The board generally delegates its financial reporting oversight function to the audit committee, with the full board maintaining responsibility and accountability for the delegated function. The board normally establishes the audit committee to assist in effectively fulfilling its fiduciary duty of protecting investor interests with the keen understanding that the entire board is responsible for the company's oversight function.

The audit committee should regularly report its activities to the board of directors and get board approvals for its agendas. Although many audit committees may employ self-evaluating mechanisms for their performance, the board of directors is ultimately responsible for the annual evaluation of the audit committee and its members.

Audit Committee Interaction with Other Board Standing Committees

In order to better discharge its responsibilities, an audit committee often will work with other standing committees of the board of directors. These other committees may include governance, compensation, finance, budget, investment, and the nominating committee. Productive working relationships among the audit committee and other standing board committees can greatly assist a board of directors in effectively coordinating its overall oversight functions. The audit committee's understanding of executive compensation and incentive plans can assist the audit committee in assessing management's motivations for aggressive earnings management or the use of aggressive accounting policies and practices for meeting earnings targets. The relationship between the audit committee and nominating committee can help in assessing professional qualifications, personal integrity, ethical behavior, and the management and operating style of senior executives, as well as the leadership philosophy of directors. The audit committee's relationship with other standing committees of the board is explored below.

Audit Committee Interaction with Compensation Committee

Public companies should establish a compensation committee with a written charter specifying the purpose and responsibilities of the committee. The purpose of the compensation committee is to assist the board in establishing fair and rewarding compensation for the company's directors and officers. Responsibilities of the compensation committee are to: (1) establish a compensation plan consistent with the company's goals; (2) recommend to the board of directors the CEO's compensation; (3) recommend to the board a non-CEO compensation plan; and (4) prepare the compensation committee report to be included in the proxy statement. The compensation committee can play an important role in corporate governance because of substantial increases in executive compensation during the past several years and public interest in and scrutiny of executive compensation. The audit committee should interact with the compensation committee to obtain an understanding of executive compensation and incentive plans and their impact on the fair presentation of the company's financial statements. The audit committee may interact with the compensation committee in several ways: (1) both committees are mandatory standing board committees, and, as such, participate in activities requiring the entire board's deliberation; (2) the compensation committee may seek the advice of the audit committee pertaining to the tax, audit, and reporting requirements of directors' and officers' compensation plans (long-term incentive plans, stock options); (3) the entire board, including the audit committee, normally evaluates the performance of mandatory standing board committees; and (4) in a small-sized board (e.g., less than seven directors), an audit committee member may also serve on the compensation committee.

Audit Committee Interaction with Nominating Committee

Public companies should establish a nominating committee comprised solely of independent directors. The nominating governance committee should have a written charter specifying the purpose and responsibility of the committee. Suggested oversight functions and responsibilities of the nominating governance committee are to: (1) recruit candidates qualified for board membership according to board-approved criteria; (2) identify the qualifications and expertise needs of the board of directors; (3) select and recommend nominees to the board of directors; (4) present the selected director nominees at the next annual shareholders meeting; (5) establish and recommend to the board of directors a set of appropriate corporate governance principles; (6) participate with other committees of the board (compensation, audit) in the evaluation of the board and management; and (7) submit the committee's annual report to the board.

The nominating committee should also nominate candidates for the audit committee and assist the board of directors in appointing audit committee members. Although legally permissible, the appointment of audit committee members by the company's CEO may compromise the member's objectivity and independence. The audit committee often assists the board of directors in evaluating members of the nominating committee. In a board of directors with a small number of directors (fewer than seven) and several standing committees (more than two), a director may serve on both the audit committee and the nominating/governance committee. A collegial relationship between the nominating and audit committees can improve the effectiveness of both. Nevertheless, no director should chair both committees.

Audit Committee Interaction with Management

An effective audit committee oversight function requires considerable interaction with management and can only be achieved by an audit committee forging a close working relationship with management. The audit committee oversees financial reporting, internal controls, and risk assessment functions. Management should provide the audit committee with adequate information involving the financial condition, results of operations, financial statements, estimates, reserves, accruals, financial reporting risk assessment, internal control over financial reporting, significant deficiencies, material weaknesses in internal controls, and management's interactions with both internal and external auditors.

A close working relationship between management and the audit committee can substantially improve the effectiveness of corporate governance. The audit committee may meet privately with management, particularly financial managers, to discuss matters pertaining to the appointment and evaluation of the independent auditor, the appointment, compensation, and evaluation of internal auditors, internal controls, risk assessment, whistle-blower programs, and the financial reporting process.

Audit Committee Interaction with Internal and External Auditors

Audit committees have traditionally been formed primarily to function as a liaison between management and auditors to preserve the auditors' independence. This role remains essential. However, recent corporate governance reforms (SOX, SEC rules, listing standards, best practices) have expanded and improved the relationship between the audit committee and both internal and external auditors. The audit committee is directly responsible for appointing, retaining, compensating, and overseeing the work of the independent auditor. The audit committee is also responsible for approving all audit and permissible non-audit services in compliance with provisions of SOX 2002. This makes the independent auditor ultimately accountable to the audit committee. The audit committee is also directly responsible for hiring, firing, and compensating the chief audit executive (CAE, the director of the internal audit function) and other key internal audit personnel, as well as approving the budget, staffing, and audit plans of internal auditors. Thus, both internal and external auditors essentially work with management for the audit committee. The audit committee relationship with external and internal auditors is further discussed in Chapters 4 and 5, respectively.

Audit Committee Interaction with Legal Counsel

An audit committee should establish strong and candid relationships with the company's legal counsel (both internal general counsel and outside legal counsel). These relationships can provide the audit committee with useful information regarding any possible violations of applicable rules and regulations, noncompliance with the company's code of conduct, and high-risk business and financial areas. For example, an audit committee may learn from the company's general counsel about significant or unusual transactions that the company is contemplating. On the basis of this information, the audit committee can investigate whether these transactions will be structured or might be viewed as being structured inappropriately to manage earnings or achieve financial targets. By intervening early enough, the audit committee might prevent the company from taking steps that could otherwise result in misleading financial reports. The company's general counsel should assist the chairperson of the audit committee in preparing meeting agenda, should attend meetings of the audit committee, and should review at least the final draft reports of meetings. If possible violations of laws, rules, and regulations surface, the audit committee should work closely with legal counsel to investigate them.

Conclusion

Effective compliance with new corporate governance reforms, complexity of business, globalization, and technological advances have encouraged the board of directors to establish standing committees to best utilize the expertise, knowledge, and efforts of its committees. Several mandatory committees of the board have emerged in recent years. The three mandatory committees for listed companies are audit, nominating, and compensation committees. Other board committees, such as budget, finance, executive, special litigation, disclosure, or investment committees, may also be established by some public companies. Recent developments in corporate governance reforms have boosted the relevance, importance, and public profiles of all three mandatory committees for public companies in general and the audit committee in particular. Thus, as public companies are facing challenges in the global environment, the need for a better understanding of these committees and their activities is becoming increasingly important. Board committees are normally formed to assist the company's board of directors in effectively fulfilling its fiduciary duty of protecting investor interests with the keen understanding that the entire board is responsible for the company's oversight function. The audit committee is an integral component of corporate governance and as such interacts with other corporate governance participants including the entire board of directors, other board committees, management, internal auditors, external auditors, and legal counsel.

Action Items

1. Clearly define audit committee oversight functions in its charter.
2. Periodically review the assigned oversight functions.

3. Annually evaluate the audit committee effectiveness in achieving its oversight functions.

4. Ensure audit committee oversight functions are in compliance with all applicable laws, rules, regulations, and standards.

5. Implement best practices of audit committee oversight functions.

6. Revise the audit committee charter as the focus on the audit committee will continue in the coming years as the global initiatives address the importance of audit committees in corporate governance.

Endnotes

1. Sarbanes-Oxley Act. 2002. Section 301: Audit committee. Available at: www.sec.gov/about/laws/soa2002.pdf

2. Dodd-Frank Wall Street Reform and Consumer Protection Act of 2010. (pp. 111–203). Pub. L.

3. Securities and Exchange Commission (SEC). 2003. Disclosure Required by Section 406 and 407 of the Sarbanes-Oxley Act of 2002 (January 23). Rule No. 33-8177. Available at: www.sec.gov/rules/final/shtml

CHAPTER 2

Financial Reporting Oversight Function of the Audit Committee

Executive Summary

The financial reporting oversight function (FROF) of the audit committee includes reviewing financial communications, including financial statements and disclosures, earnings releases, earnings guidance, and overseeing management's accounting policies and practices. The FROF is the most important responsibility of the audit committee, and in most (if not all) cases, an audit committee can perform no function more significant than reviewing a company's financial reports and financial reporting processes. An audit committee's effective of FROF can improve the integrity, reliability, quality, and transparency of financial reports. The audit committee should review and discuss both annual and quarterly financial statements with the management, internal auditor, and the independent auditor and get the entire board of directors' approval of financial reports before they are disseminated to shareholders or filed with the Securities and Exchange Commission (SEC) for public companies. This chapter examines the FROF of the audit committee and the ways that the audit committee can improve the quality and quantity of financial reports.

Introduction

Management is directly responsible for the true and fair presentation of financial statements in conformity with the generally accepted accounting principles (GAAP). However, by effectively performing their assigned functions, both the company's audit committee and the independent auditor can lend credibility to financial statements. The FROF of the audit committee requires that the audit committee reviews financial communications, including financial statements and disclosures, earnings releases, and earnings guidance, and oversees audited financial statements as well as management's accounting policies and practices. The FROF enables the audit committee to : (1) assist the board in overseeing the integrity of the company's financial statements; (2) review and discuss the company's annual and quarterly financial statements with management and the external auditor; (3) discuss accounting policies and practices with management; (4) review and discuss with management the company's earnings releases and financial information and earnings guidance provided to analysts and rating agencies; and (5) review any other financial and non-financial corporate communications with management prior to dissemination to external users.

To fulfill this function, all members of the company's audit committee should be financially literate, and at least one member should be designated as the audit committee financial expert. Financial literacy means sufficient understanding of the company's financial reporting requirements including the four basic financial statements (the balance sheet, income statement, statements of retained earnings, and statement of cash flows) and required filings with the SEC (annual audited financial statements via Form 10-K and quarterly reviewed financial statements via Form 10-Q). The financial reporting oversight function of the audit committee primarily focuses on financial information contained in both annual and quarterly reports. However, the audit committee should also read the non-financial information often contained in annual reports to ensure its consistency with financial information presented in the financial statements. The audit committee should review the company's audited financial statements and recommend to the entire board of directors that they be disseminated to shareowners and filed with regulatory agencies (SEC).

Overseeing Annual Financial Statements

Recent (2014) annual reports of General Electric (GE) are used to illustrate the four basic financial statements (See Exhibit 2.1). On the basis of this background, the following section details how audit committees should oversee annual financial statements in effectively fulfilling its FROF.

Annual Reports

The annual report of public companies normally contains the following financial information:

1. Audited financial statements, including their notes.
2. Management's discussion and analysis (MD&A) of the financial condition and results of operations.
3. Management certifications of financial statements.
4. Management assessments of the effectiveness of internal control over financial reporting.
5. Audit committee report.
6. Independent auditor's report on financial statements.
7. Independent auditor's report on management assessment of the effectiveness of internal control over financial reporting.[1]
8. Five-year summary of selected financial data.
9. Summary of selected quarterly financial data for the past two years.
10. Quarterly market data for the past two years, including high and low stock prices for common stock, dividends paid, and the price-earnings ratio.

Example: General Electric

General Electric (GE) is selected as the benchmark company throughout the book, because it is ranked within the top 10 best companies' corporate governance worldwide. The IR Global Rankings ranks GE as among the top 10 companies based on management accountability, board of directors, minority shareholder protection, controlling shareholders and shareholders' meeting procedures, financial statements, and disclosure and other policies.[2] Exhibit 2.1 reproduces four basic financial statements of GE extracted from its 2013 and 2014 annual reports:

1. GE's balance sheet shows its financial position (assets, liabilities, and stockholders equity) as of December 31, 2014 and 2013.
2. GE's income statement reports the results of its operations (net income or net loss) for three consecutive years of 2014, 2013, and 2012.

Exhibit 2.1

Condensed consolidated financial statements of General Electric company

Panel A: Consolidated balance sheets as of December 31, 2014, 2013

Years ended December 31 (dollars in millions)	2014	2013
Assets		
Current Assets	$412,952	$422,303
Other Assets	235,397	234,257
Total assets	$648,349	$656,560
Liabilities and equity		
Current Liabilities	$115,663	$123,087
Long-term liabilities	395,853	396,690
Total liabilities	511,516	519,777
Shareowners' Equity		
Common stock	702	702
Accumulated other comprehensive income (loss)	(18,152)	(9,120)
Other capital	32,889	32,494
Retained earnings	112,740	106,490
Total GE shareowners' equity	128,159	130,566
Noncontrolling interests	8,674	6,217
Total equity	136,833	136,783
Total liabilities and equity	$ 648,349	$ 656,560

Panel B: Consolidated statements of income

Years Ended December 31, (dollars in millions except per share amounts)	2014	2013	2012
Total revenues and other income	$148,589	$146,045	$146,684
Costs and expenses			
Cost of goods sold	61,257	57,867	56,785
Other costs and expenses	70,103	72,027	72,518
Total costs and expenses	131,360	129,894	129,303
Net income before tax	17,229	16,151	17,381
Benefit (provision) for income taxes	(1,772)	(676)	(2,534)

Earnings from continuing operations	15,457	15,475	14,847
Earnings (loss) from discontinued operations	(112)	(2,120)	(983)
Net earnings	15,345	13,355	13,864

Panel C: Consolidated statements of cash flows

For the Years Ended December 31,	2014	2013	2012
Cash flows – operating activities	27,710	28,579	31,331
Cash flows – investing activities	(5,030)	29,117	11,302
Cash flows – financing activities	(16,958)	(45,573)	(51,074)

Panel D: Consolidated statements of changes in stockholders' equity

(dollars in millions)	2014	2013	2012
GE shareowners' equity balance at January 1	130,566	123,026	116,438
Net Income	15,233	13,057	13,641
Dividends	(8,951)	(8,061)	(7,372)
Changes in other capital	16	(8,761)	(5,763)
Total equity balance at December 31	136,833	136,783	128,470

Source: Adapted from GE's Annual Report Available at: www.ge.com/ar2014/assets/pdf/ GE_AR14.pdf

3. GE's statement of cash flows reports its operating, investing, and financing cash flow activities as well as changes in its cash accounts for three consecutive years of 2014, 2013, and 2012.

4. GE's statement of stockholders' equity reports the changes in its stockholders' equity accounts including retained earnings for three consecutive years of 2014, 2013, and 2012.

   a. Balance Sheet

   GE's balance sheet as of December 31, 2014 shows its total assets of $648,349 million (reflecting its economic resources), total liabilities of $511,516 million (representing its creditors' claims to the assets), and stockholders' equity of $136,833 million. GE's total assets include: (1) cash and equivalents; (2) investment securities; (3) current receivables; (4) inventories; (5) financing receivables; (6) property, plant, and equipment; (7) investment in

General Electric Capital Corporation (GECC); (8) Goodwill and other intangible assets; (9) deferred income taxes; (10) assets of businesses held for sale; and (11) assets of discontinued operations.

GE's total liabilities of $511,516 million consist of: (1) short-term borrowings; (2) accounts payable; (3) progress collections and price adjustments accrued; (4) dividends payable; (5) non-recourse borrowings of consolidated securitization entities; (6) bank deposits; (7) long-term borrowings; (8) investment contracts, insurance liabilities, and insurance annuity benefits; (9) liabilities of businesses held for sale; and (10) liabilities of discontinued operations.

GE's total stockholders' equity of $136,833 million consists of: (1) common stock showing its shareholders' contributions up to the par value of $702 million in stock; (2) accumulated other comprehensive income (including investment securities, currency translation adjustments, cash flow hedges, and benefit plans); (3) retained earnings of $155,333 million; (4) other capital of $32,889 million; and (5) common stock held in treasury of 42,593 million.

b. Income Statement

GE's income statement for the year ended December 31, 2014 shows: (1) its total revenues of $148,589 million in 2014; (2) total expenses of $131,360 million incurred in generating revenues; (3) net income of $15,233 million; and (4) earnings per share $1.50.

c. Statement of Cash Flows

GE's statement of cash flows for the year ended December 31, 2014 consists of four parts: (1) Cash inflows and outflows and net cash flows of $27,710 million resulting from operating activities such as selling goods, buying raw materials, paying wages pertaining to its main operations and productions; (2) Cash inflows and cash outflows, and net cash flows of $(5,030) million pertaining to investing activities primarily in productive assets; (3) Cash provided from and used for, and net cash flows of $(16,958) million related to financing activities of issues stock and incurring debts; and (4) Net cash flows that increase the beginning balance of cash account by $2,230 million.

d. Statement of Stockholders Equity

GE's statement of stockholders' equity for the year ended December 31, 2014 shows the changes in stockholders' equity and retained earnings for 2014. This statement includes the beginning balance of stockholders' equity, any increases from net earnings attributable to the company, dividends and other transactions with shareowners, other comprehensive incomes (foreign currency translation adjustments, unrealized gains on derivatives, unrealized losses on securities, minimum pension liability adjustment), net sales of shares for treasury, changes in other capital, and finally the total ending balance of stockholder's equity.

Notes to Financial Statements

Footnotes accompanying the financial statements are integral components of financial statements and typically follow immediately after the financial statements. These notes are classified into two main categories: (1) The summary of significant accounting policies and practices used by management in measuring, recognizing, and reporting financial items presented in the financial statements; and (2) More detailed information about significant financial items.

Management's Discussion and Analysis

Supplementing basic financial statements and the accompanying notes, MD&A of financial condition, and the results of operations is intended to provide a narrative explanation of financial information. This information, which the SEC requires, is designed to assist investors in assessing the quality of the company's earnings and future growth and prospects. SEC Financial Reporting Release No. 72, "Interpretation: Commission Guidance Reporting Management's Discussion and Analysis of Financial Condition and Results of Operations," provides MD&A guidance in four areas: (1) The overall presentation of MD&A; (2) The general content of MD&A; (3) Disclosures regarding liquidity and capital resources; and (4) Disclosures pertaining to critical accounting estimates.[3]

Overseeing Annual Audited Financial Statements

In the post–Sarbanes–Oxley Act of 2002 (SOX) era, the audit committee is directly responsible for pre-approving audit and non-audit services and overseeing the work of the independent auditor, particularly as related to audited financial statements. Prior to the passage of SOX, the Statement on Auditing Standards (SAS) No. 61 of the AICPA and Communications with Audit Committees (as amended by SAS Nos. 89 and 90) provided guidance for the interaction between the audit committee and the independent auditor.[4] SAS No. 61 requires the independent auditor to communicate the following matters with audit clients' audit committee:

A) Independent auditor responsibilities under generally accepted auditing standards (GAAS): For public companies, the independent auditors should communicate their responsibilities under professional standards adopted by the Public Company Accounting Oversight Board (PCAOB), United States.
B) The client company's significant accounting policies.
C) Management's significant judgments and accounting estimates.
D) Audit adjustments recorded and those not recorded.
E) Independent auditor judgments about the quality of accounting principles used by management in the preparation of financial statements.
F) Other information in documents containing audited financial statements.
G) Disagreements with management.
H) Consultations with other accountants.
I) Difficulties encountered in performing the audit.
J) Important issues discussed with management prior to retention of the independent auditor.

SOX created a more appropriate balance of power-sharing between management and the audit committee as related to the audited financial statements by changing the audit committee's relationship and interaction with the independent auditor in several ways. First, Section 301 of SOX requires the audit committee to be directly responsible for the appointment, compensation, retention, and oversight of the work of the independent auditor. This practically considers the audit committee, not management, as the client of the independent auditor, which means the independent auditor works with management for the audit committee. Second, Section 202 of SOX requires the audit committee to preapprove all audit and permissible non-audit services to be performed by the independent auditor, which practically reduces potential conflicts of interest between management and the independent auditor by granting the authority to engage the independent auditor to the audit committee. Finally, Section 204 of SOX and the SEC's final rule require the independent auditor to communicate either orally or in written form as frequently as needed, preferably on a continuous basis, if not quarterly, or definitely before filing the annual financial report with the SEC, the following matters:

1. All critical accounting policies and practices used by the company in the preparation of financial statements.
2. All alternative accounting treatments within generally accepted accounting principles for accounting policies and procedures relevant to material financial items and transactions that have been discussed with management. This should include the ramifications of the use of such alternative accounting treatments and disclosures as well as the treatment preferred by the independent auditor.
3. Other material written communications between the independent auditors and management.

In addition to the above communications required by SAS No. 61, SOX, and the SEC rules, listing standards of national stock exchanges require:[5] (1) the public accounting firm to communicate to the company's audit committee its relationships with the company, its quality control procedures, and the results of quality control reviews and investigations; and (2) the audit committee establish the appropriate hiring policies for current employees or former employees of the company's public accounting firm and communicate such policies to the independent auditor. PCAOB Auditing Standard No. 2 also requires the independent auditor to communicate significant deficiencies and material weaknesses in internal control over financial reporting to the company's audit committee.

The author suggests that public companies: (1) in complying with the emerging corporate governance reforms related to the interaction between the audit committee, management, and the independent auditor, establish an appropriate, balanced, effective working relationship, and a mutual respect and cooperation between all participants in the financial reporting supply chain including the audit committee, management, independent auditor, internal auditor, and legal counsel; (2) ensure that their audit committee has the authority and direct responsibility to appoint, compensate, terminate, and oversee the work of the independent auditors; (3) seek shareholder ratification of the independent auditor appointment in their annual proxies; (4) maintain formal and informal, oral or written, open lines of communication between their independent auditor and the audit committee on a continuous basis to discuss all issues and concerns relevant to financial reporting and audit activities; (4) manage private meetings between independent auditor and the audit committee as frequently as needed or at least quarterly; (5) establish policies and procedures for their audit committee to pre-approve all audit and permissible non-audit services to be provided by the independent auditor; and (6) establish appropriate policies and procedures for the employment of current or former employees of their public accounting firm that comply with SOX provisions, SEC rules, and listing standards.

The audit committee and particularly the designated audit committee financial expert should review the content of financial statements and accompanying information and pay particular attention to the following items in the annual audited financial statements:

Critical Accounting Policies and Practices

Management should communicate with the audit committee important accounting policies and practices used in the preparation of financial reports. External auditors should discuss and confirm that management has effectively and sufficiently communicated the company's accounting policies, practices, and estimates with the audit committee. Section 204 of SOX requires that the independent auditor make timely reports to the audit committee regarding all critical accounting policies and practices used by management in the measurement, recognition of business transactions and events, and the final preparation of the financial statements.[6]

The audit committee should review their reports and discuss them with the company's independent auditor to ensure that proper accounting policies and practices are being used. Particular attention should be paid to complex areas such as asset valuation (fair value determination) and revenue recognition, expense estimation (depreciation), and related-party transactions.

Initial Adoption of Accounting Policies and Changes in Existing Policies

Accounting policies consist of accounting principles and methods that management uses in measuring, recognizing, and reporting financial transactions and in preparing financial statements. Public companies must apply GAAP as accounting policies in their financial reporting. Public companies initially adopt an accounting policy when: (1) accounting standard-setting bodies promulgate new financial reporting standards that supersede the prior standards; (2) business transactions and events affecting the company's financial position or results of operations occur for the first time; (3) significant changes in the content and nature of business events and transactions; and (4) business transactions and events previously considered immaterial begin to materially affect financial reporting. The initial adoption of accounting policies or changes in the existing accounting policies should be communicated to the audit committee. If they materially affect the company's financial presentation (financial condition and results of operations), then these changes should also be disclosed to shareholders. The audit committee should review the significant accounting policies used by the company and assess whether they are appropriate, reasonable, and justifiable under the circumstances. Management and the independent auditor should inform audit committee members of changes in accounting policies including accounting and reporting standards, particularly new accounting standards and their possible impacts on the company's financial statements.

Accounting Estimates and Reserves

It is important that management defines and discusses with the audit committee the threshold for significant accounting estimates, reserves and unusual transactions and their related judgments. Significant accounting issues and estimates as well as significant unusual transactions and judgments that should be communicated with the audit committee are those that: (1) cause controversy among executives (chief executive officers [CEOs], chief financial officers [CFOs], controllers, and treasures) and between executives and internal and external auditors; (2) lack authoritative guidelines and for which the consensus cannot be reached; (3) have material impacts on the quality and quality of financial reports; (4) have potential to discover and correct errors, irregularities, and fraud; and (5) can impact internal control over financial reporting (ICFR). Accounting estimates and reserves that materially affect the company's financial condition and results of operations should be properly communicated to the audit committee. Examples include pension expenses, postretirement expenses, net realized value of inventories, useful life of plants and equipments, loan loss, asset impairments, and uncollectible accounts receivable. The independent auditor and the CFO should explain to the audit committee the methods used and assumptions made in accounting estimates and reserves, and the audit committee should satisfy itself with management's basis and justifications for such estimates and reserves. Accounting estimates, accruals, and reserves require management to predict the effects of events that might occur in the long term. Accordingly, the audit committee should obtain timely information about these events and whether they are reflected in the financial statements. In reviewing accounting estimates, reserves, and accruals, the audit committee should: (1) consider the reliability and reasonableness of data underlying the estimate; (2) appropriateness and quality of the methods and systems used to determine estimates, reserves, and accruals; and (3) understand the reasons for reporting the timing and amounts of estimates, reserves, and accruals. The audit committee should be proactive and consistent in asking questions and discuss with management regarding significant accounting issues, policies, practices, estimates, and judgments.

Significant Changes in the Content and Format of Financial Statement Presentation

In reviewing the content and format of financial statements, the audit committee should pay special attention to financial items (assets, liabilities, revenues, expenses) that have changed substantially (increased or decreased) in comparison to prior years or other benchmarks (industry norms). The audit committee should also discuss with management (CFO) and the independent auditors unusual transactions and related-party transactions, as well as significant changes in the format of financial statement presentation and receive satisfactory explanations for these changes. The audit committee should review significant period-to-period changes in all financial items and demand satisfactory explanations for significant variances between the actual performance and the planned budgets.

End of the Year Transactions, and Audit Classifications
and Audit Adjustments

The audit committee should review and discuss with both management and the independent auditor significant adjusting and reclassification entries that occur at or near the end of a quarter or year and satisfy itself about management justifications and reasons for those transactions. Examples of these transactions are allowances for doubtful accounts, estimated depreciation expenses, unusual end of the period revenue, and expense transactions. The audit committee also should review significant adjustments, reclassifications, disclosures suggested by the independent auditor, management's response to those transactions or events, all the recorded adjustments and unrecorded adjustments, and management's reasons and justifications for not recording them. Examples are errors discovered by the independent auditor during the audit of financial statements that are considered to be material and affect true and fair presentation of the financial statements in conformity with GAAP. These discovered errors reflect misstatements in the financial statements and should be reviewed and corrected before the financial statements are released to shareholders or filed with the SEC. Failure to correct these errors may cause misleading financial statements and subsequent costly restatements of already published financial statements. The audit committee should be satisfied with management's and the independent auditor's justifications, reasons, and rationale for recorded and unrecorded adjustments and their impact on financial statement presentation.

Independent Auditor Disagreements with Management on Accounting Matters

The independent auditor should advise the company's audit committee regarding any disagreements with management regarding financial statement presentation and disclosures. The audit committee should review these disagreements, seek consultation, and resolve the matters in a manner that would not materially affect the fair presentation of financial statements in conformity with GAAP. For example, the independent auditor may disagree with management regarding classification of an expenditure as an expense or the timing of its recognition, or management may disagree with the independent auditor's classification of the discovered weaknesses in internal control as material weaknesses requiring public disclosures as opposed to significant deficiencies requiring disclosure to the audit committee. In these circumstances, the audit committee should review the disagreements and resolve the disputed issues in a manner that prevents misleading financial information.

Off-Balance Sheet and Related-Party Transactions

Section 401(c) of SOX directs the SEC to conduct a study to determine: (1) the extent of off-balance sheet transactions including assets, liabilities, leases, losses, and the use of special purpose entities by public companies; and (2) whether existing accounting policies and practices properly reflect the economics of such off-balance sheet transactions and provide relevant and transparent information to investors.[7] The SEC conducted its study and identified several major initiatives to improve transparency in financial reporting, including: (1) discouraging transactions and transaction structures primarily motivated by accounting and recording concerns rather than economics; (2) expanding the use of objectives-oriented standards to make off-balance sheet transactions more transparent; (3) improving the consistency and relevance of disclosures; and (4) improving the communication focus in financial reporting.[8] The SEC also suggests additional guidance by the Financial Accounting Standards Board (FASB) to address some of the concerns with the failure of companies to consolidate certain special purpose entities.[9] The listing standards of AMEX require the audit committee to review and approve all significant related-party transactions.[10] Management is primarily responsible for defining related parties and identifying significant related-party transactions. The audit committee should review the business reasons for such transactions and whether these reasons are aligned with the company's overall sustainable objectives and strategic decisions and their impacts on the financial statements. The audit committee should review and discuss with both management and the independent auditor proper identification and disclosure of both off-balance sheet transactions and related-party transactions.

Overseeing Interim Reviewed Financial Statements

Besides reviewing a company's annual financial report, an audit committee also plays an important role overseeing interim financial statements. SEC rules require that interim (quarterly) financial statements of public companies under its jurisdiction be reviewed by the company's independent auditor before those statements are filed with the Commission.[11] The independent auditor typically performs limited work (inquiries, analytical procedures) on interim financial statements and may identify material departures and/or misstatements from GAAP. The independent auditor should advise the company's audit committee about possible misstatements in the interim financial statements and ask management to take proper action(s) to correct them. The audit committee should also ask management whether interim reports are performed on a basis consistent with annual financial statements and whether management judgments and estimates were appropriate.

In its auditor's review report accompanying interim financial statements, the independent auditor often states that it is not aware of any modifications that should be made to the financial statements to make them in conformity with GAAP. This level of assurance, commonly referred to as a negative assurance, is lower than that of financial statement audit and provides no basis to express an opinion (reasonable assurance) that financial statements are free from material misstatement caused by error or fraud. Before interim financial statements are issued, the audit committee should ask the independent auditor to identify those items with respect to which the auditor proposes to provide merely reasonable assurance. The audit committee should then ascertain by conversing with both the independent auditor and management that the financial statements will be free from material misstatement caused by error or fraud.

To ensure quality, reliability, integrity, and transparency of financial information provided to investors, companies require that quarterly earnings releases be reviewed by several participants in the corporate governance financial reporting supply chain including the full board and audit committee, internal auditors, external auditors, general counsel, and disclosure committee. The Deloitte and Touche 2003 survey indicates that the majority of surveyed companies had their quarterly earnings releases prior to public issuance reviewed by the full audit committee including the chairperson, internal auditors, disclosure committee, and the general counsel.[12] The majority of companies also had their 10-Q reviewed by the full audit committee, internal auditors, disclosure committees, and general counsel prior to its filing with the SEC.[13] The small minority (about 10 percent) had both their quarterly earnings releases and 10-Q filings reviewed by the entire board of directors.[14] These results suggest an increasing trend toward the review of both 10-Q filings and quarterly earnings releases by the entire audit committee, internal auditors, disclosure committee, and legal counsel prior to their public release. Of course, the 10-Q filings are required to be reviewed by independent auditors, and auditors should provide a review report on quarterly financial statements filed with the SEC. The auditor's review report on quarterly financial statements is attached to the filing of quarterly financial statements (Form 10-Q), whereas the annual audit of financial statements is filed with the annual financial statements on Form 10-K.

Management Certifications of Financial Reports and Internal Controls

Two provisions of SOX pertain to management certifications of financial reports. Section 302 of the Act requires the principal executive and financial officers of the company (CEO, CFO) to certify each periodic (quarterly and annual) report filed with the SEC.[15] This is also referred to as the civil certification, because the certifying officers may face civil actions for false certification. Under section 906 of the Act, each periodic report containing financial statements filed by a reporting company must be accompanied by a certification of the CEO and CFO of the company.[16] This certification is viewed as the criminal certification because the certifying officers also face criminal penalties for filing false financial statements. ICFR is a process designed by management to provide reasonable assurance pertaining to the reliability of the company's financial reporting and preparation of financial statements in accordance with GAAP. Management is required to annually assess and certify ICFR and report on its effectiveness, and the external auditor must conduct an audit of ICFR as part of its integrated audit. Management (CEO and CFO) is also required to make quarterly certifications regarding the effectiveness of ICFR, as well as the company's disclosure controls and procedures. The audit committee should have regular discussions with management and external and internal auditors regarding the status of the company's ICFR, including the status of audits and certification processes.

On June 27, 2007, the SEC issued Interpretive Guidance (IG) and rule amendments to assist public companies' compliance with Section 404.[17] The IG provides guidance for management on how to conduct an assessment of the effectiveness of ICFR. The IG suggests management use a top-down, risk-based approach in evaluating ICFR and in satisfying the annual evaluation requirement in Exchange Act Rules 13a-15(c) and 15d-15(c). Exhibit 2.2 suggests a sample executive certification of annual reports. Section 302 of the SOX requires that executive certification is signed by both the company's CEO and CFO. As indicated in Exhibit 2.3, both certifying officers (CEO and CFO) certify that:

1. Financial reports (quarterly and annual) are reviewed by them.
2. Financial reports are materially accurate and complete.
3. On the basis of their knowledge, financial statements including footnotes and other financial information including selected financial data, MD&A analysis of financial condition, and results of operations contained in the report fairly present in all material respects the company's financial condition, results of operations, and cash flows. The fair presentation of financial reports including financial statements and other financial information is broader than fair presentation of financial statements under GAAP.

Exhibit 2.2

Executive certification of annual report

I, Z. Rezaee, certify that:

1. I have reviewed this annual report on Form 10-K of NRZ Inc.
2. To the best of my knowledge, this annual report does not contain any untrue statements.
3. To the best of my knowledge, the financial statements and other financial information included in this annual fairly presented in all material respects the financial condition and results of operation and cash flows.
4. The company's other certifying officers and I are responsible for establishing and maintaining disclosure controls and procedures as defined in Exchange Act Rules 13a-15(e) and 15d-15(e).
5. The company's other certifying officers and I have disclosed, based on our assessment of ICFR, to the company's audit committee and the independent auditor:
    a. All significant deficiencies and material weaknesses in the design and operation of ICFR.
    b. Any fraud involving management or other employees who have a significant role in the company's ICFR and financial reports.

Date: January 25, 2015   Signature: Z. Rezaee

Title: Chairman and Chief Executive

4. The certifying officers: (a) are responsible for establishing and maintaining the company's "disclosure controls and procedures" and "internal control over financial reporting"; (b) have assessed the effectiveness of the company's disclosure controls and procedures within 90 days prior to the filing of the report; (c) have presented in the report their conclusions about the effectiveness of disclosure controls and procedures.
5. The certifying officers (CEO and CFO) have disclosed to the company's independent auditors and the audit committee of the board of directors: (a) all significant deficiencies and material weaknesses in the design and operations of the ICFR; (b) any fraud

Exhibit 2.3

General Electric Company

Management's annual report on internal control over financial reporting

Management is responsible for establishing and maintaining adequate internal control over financial reporting for the Company. With our participation, an evaluation of the effectiveness of our internal control over financial reporting was conducted as of December 31, 2014, based on the framework and criteria established in Internal Control ± Integrated Framework (2013) issued by the Committee of Sponsoring Organizations of the Treadway Commission.

Based on this evaluation, our management has concluded that our internal control over financial reporting was effective as of December 31, 2014.

Our independent registered public accounting firm has issued an audit report on our internal control over financial reporting. Their report follows.

/s/ Jeffrey R. Immelt	/s/ Jeffrey S. Bornstein
Jeffrey R. Immelt	Jeffrey S. Bornstein
Chairman of the Board and	Senior Vice President and
Chief Executive Officer	Chief Financial Officer
February 27, 2015	

that involves management or other employees with a significant role in ICFR.

The integrity and efficient function of the capital markets depend on the quality of financial information disseminated to the financial markets by public companies. The audit committee must oversee the quality, reliability, and transparency of published financial statements. One of the important (if not most important) oversight functions of the audit committee is to oversee the company's financial reporting process including both annual financial statements and quarterly financial statements and earnings releases. Public companies disclose a great deal of financial information in addition to interim and annual financial statements to the public. The audit committee should oversee the fairness, reliability, quality, and transparency of such disclosures.

Audit Committee Role in ICSR

The audit committee should oversee the adequacy and effectiveness of the company's internal control structure to assure: (a) the efficiency and effectiveness of operations; (b) the reliability of financial reporting; and (c) compliance with applicable laws and regulations. The committee's oversight of Section 404 on internal control is becoming more important as public companies are required to certify their ICFR. The audit committee should: (1) know the senior executive who is directly responsible and ultimately accountable for Section 404 compliance; (2) understand the process of establishing and maintaining adequate and effective internal control; (3) understand procedures for assessing the effectiveness of both the design and operation of ICFR; (4) understand the proper documentation of compliance with Section 404; (5) review management's report on the effectiveness of ICFR; (6) review auditor reports expressing an opinion on management's assessment of the effectiveness of ICFR; (7) evaluate the identified significant deficiencies and material weaknesses in internal control; (8) be satisfied with management and auditor efforts and reports on ICFR; and (9) ensure that management has properly addressed the identified material weaknesses.

The American Institute of Certified Public Accountants (AICPA), in February 2005, issued a report titled *Management Override of Internal Controls: The Achilles' Heel of Fraud Prevention*.[18] This report is part of an ongoing effort of the AICPA in providing guidance to audit committees to effectively oversee their company's internal controls and address the risk of management override of ICFR. The guidelines provided in the report were intended to assist audit committees to prevent, deter, and detect fraudulent financial reporting. Management is primarily responsible for the design and operation of adequate and effective ICFR. However, there is always the risk that management may override internal controls, which makes the otherwise effective internal controls inoperative. The audit committee should be aware of such a risk and address the likelihood of its occurrence in overseeing the company's financial reporting.

The AICPA report indicates that management may override internal control and engage in financial statement fraud by: (1) recording fictitious business transactions and events or altering the timing of recognition of legitimate transactions; (2) recording and reversing biased reserves through unjustifiable estimates and judgments; and (3) changing the records and terms of significant or unusual transactions.[19] The report offers several recommendations and actions that can be taken by audit committees to address the risk of management override of ICFR.

The suggested actions for addressing and assessing financial statements fraud risk caused by management override of internal controls are: (1) exercising an appropriate level of skepticism; (2) strengthening the audit committee's understanding and knowledge of the company's business and industry to identify and assess business and financial risks that increase the likelihood of financial statement fraud; (3) brainstorming and open discussion among members of the audit committee about the potential for fraud including identification of events and transactions that are most likely to be susceptible to fraud, management motivations to engage in fraud, opportunities provided to management to override internal control or perpetuate fraud, and corporate culture and environment that enable management to rationalize the commission of fraud; (4) establishing and using the business code of conduct to assess financial culture by ensuring that management practices and promotes an "appropriate tone at the top" of promoting ethical behavior and legal conduct throughout the company; (5) cultivating a vigorous whistleblower program including a telephone hotline to receive tips regarding fraud and concerns pertaining to accounting and internal controls from employees, suppliers, customers, and others; and (6) establishing a broad information and feedback network that extends beyond senior management and requires the audit committee to communicate with the internal auditor, independent auditors, compensation committee, and key employees regarding the likelihood of occurrence of fraud, and how to prevent and detect fraud.[20]

The audit committee is responsible for addressing internal control activities and issues and for asking the following questions:

1. What are the internal control priorities?
2. Are there adequate internal control investments?
3. Are internal control resources properly allocated?
4. Is the company getting the right return for its investment in internal control?
5. Are entity-level controls adequate and effective?
6. Are process-level controls adequate and effective?
7. Have management and the independent auditor coordinated their plans to implement the requirements of the SEC's Interpretive Guidance and PCAOB AS No. 5?
8. Are the design and operation of ICFR effective?
9. Are the design and operation of internal control over operational performance (ICOP) effective?
10. Are the design and operation of internal control over compliance functions (ICCF) effective?
11. Is the management report on ICFR appropriate?
12. Is the independent auditor's report on ICFR appropriate?
13. What are the causes and effects of reported material weaknesses in ICFR?
14. What, if any, remediating actions have been taken or are planned by management to correct reported material weaknesses?
15. Has the independent auditor issued a report on management corrections of the reported material weaknesses?
16. What are the effects of internal control significant deficiencies and material weaknesses on potential misstatements in financial statements?

Conclusion

The FROF of the audit committee is set forth in its charter and is approved by the company's board of directors. The FROF is the most important oversight function of the audit committee and as such the members of the audit committee should be financially literate and at least one member must be designated as financial expert. An effective performance of FROF can improve the integrity, reliability, quality, and transparency of financial reports. Although management is directly responsible for true and fair presentation of financial statements in conformity with GAAP, both the company's audit committee and the independent auditor can lend credibility to financial statements. The effective oversight of the company's financial process is the most important responsibility of the audit committee. In fulfilling this oversight responsibility, the audit committee reviews the following:

1. The soundness of the financial reporting process in compliance with applicable laws, rules, regulations, and accounting standards.
2. The adequacy and competency of finance personnel as well as their expertise and knowledge of the financial reporting process and related standards and regulations.
3. The sufficiency and effectiveness of internal control over financial reporting in producing high-quality, reliable and transparent financial reports.
4. Management accounting policies and practices that are most suitable for the company's circumstances and environment.
5. Financial and non-financial disclosures including financial footnotes communicated to users of financial statements.
6. Internal audit function that assists everyone in the company to work toward achievement of the company's goals including its financial reporting objectives.
7. External audit function in lending more credibility and objectivity to published financial statements.

Action Items

1. Review financial statements including notes to the financial statements.
2. Assist the board in overseeing the integrity of the company's financial statements.
3. Review and discuss the company's annual and quarterly financial statements with management and the external auditor.

4. Discuss the company's earnings releases and financial information and earnings guidance provided to analysts and rating agencies

5. Review management certification of financial statements and internal control over financial reporting.

6. Review the completeness, accuracy, and reliability of audited financial statements and their approval of the board of directors.

7. Review the adequacy and effectiveness of internal control over financial reporting and its approval by the board of directors.

8. Review management disclosure policies and practices pertaining to financial and non-financial reports.

9. Understand unusual and complex accounting and reporting issues and how management addresses them.

10. Ensure compliance with all applicable laws, rules, regulations, standards relevant to accounting and reporting.

Endnotes

1. The independent auditor may issue an integrated report which combines items 6 & 7 in one comprehensive report on both financial statements and internal control.

2. Corporate Eye. 2008. Best Companies Corporate Governance. Available at: www.corporate-eye.com/main/best-companies-corporate-governance/

3. Securities and Exchange Commission (SEC). 2003. Financial Reporting Release No. 72: "Interpretation: Commission Guidance Reporting Management's Discussion and Analysis of Financial Condition and Results of Operations." Release No. 33-8350 (December 19). Available at: www.sec.gov/. Since 2003, the SEC has supplemented its guidance on MD&A. For details see APP, Management's Discussion and Analysis.

4. American Institute of Public Accountants (AICPA). 1988. Auditing Standards Board (ASB). Statement on Auditing Standards (SAS) No. 61. Communications with Audit Committees. Available at: www.aicpa.org

5. See Worksheets 8-12 for details of these requirements.

6. Sarbanes-Oxley Act. 2002. Section 204: Auditor Reports to Audit Committees. Available at: www.sec.gov/about/laws/soa2002.pdf

7. SOX, 2002. Section 401(c), Public Law No. 107.204
8. Securities and Exchange Commission (SEC). 2005. Report and Recommendations Pursuant to Section 401(c) of the Sarbanes-Oxley Act of 2002 on Arrangements with Off-Balance Sheet Implications. Special Purpose Entities and Transparency of Filings by Issuers. Available at: www.sec.gov/news/studies/soxoffbalancerpt.pdf
9. Financial Accounting Standards Board (FASB). 2003. Consolidation of Variable Interest Entities (revised) and Interpretation of ARB No. 51 (December). Available at: www.fasb.org
10. AMEX. 2004. Listing Standards, also see Worksheet 12.
11. Securities and Exchange Commission (SEC). 1977. The Report of the SEC Advisory Committee on Corporate Disclosure. Available at: www.sec.gov
12. Deloitte & Touche. 2003. Audit committee Financial Expert Designation and Disclosure Practice Survey. Available at: www2.financialexecutives.org/download/acbrief_8_04_03.pdf
13. Ibid.
14. Ibid.
15. Sarbanes-Oxley Act. 2002. Section 302: Corporate Responsibility for Financial Reports. Available at: www.sec.gov/about/laws/soa2002.pdf
16. Sarbanes-Oxley Act. 2002. Section 906: Corporate Responsibility for Financial Reports. Available at: www.sec.gov/about/laws/soa2002.pdf
17. Securities and Exchange Commission (SEC). 2007. Amendments to Rules Regarding Management's Report on Internal Control over Financial Reporting (June 20). Available at: www.sec.gov/rules/final/2007/33-8809.pdf
18. The American Institute of Certified Public Accountants (AICPA). 2005. Management Override of Internal Controls: The Achilles' Heel of Fraud Prevention (February). Available at: www.businesswire.com/portal/binary/com.epicentric.contentmanagement.servlet.ContentDeliveryServlet/services/ir_and_pr/ir_resource_center/editorials/2005/AICPA.pdf
19. Ibid.
20. Ibid.

CHAPTER 3

External Auditor Oversight Function of the Audit Committee

Executive Summary

Audits of financial statements and internal control over financial reporting (ICFR), in the aftermath of the Sarbanes–Oxley Act (SOX) of 2002, have played a significant role in the financial market by lending more credibility and reliability to public financial information used by investors in making sound investment decisions to make our capital market efficient. The Public Company Accounting Oversight Board (PCAOB) was created by SOX as the regulatory overseer of the public auditing profession. The audit committee and the independent auditor share a common goal of lending credibility, objectivity, dependability, and impartiality to the company's published financial statements. To achieve this goal, the audit committee and the independent auditor should have a close and productive working relationship. The audit committee has a responsibility to oversee the quality, integrity, objectivity, and transparency of financial reports. The independent auditor, in auditing those statements, has a responsibility to provide reasonable assurance that they are free from material misstatements whether caused by errors or by fraud. This chapter describes the external auditor oversight function of the audit committee to enhance the credibility of financial statements audited by the independent auditor.

Introduction

The SOX Act also put the audit committee rather than the management in charge of hiring, firing, compensating, and overseeing the work of the company's independent auditors.[1] Emerging corporate governance reforms, including SOX and Securities and Exchange Commission (SEC) implementing rules, have made the audit committee directly responsible for hiring, compensating, firing, and overseeing the work of the independent auditor, and have held the independent auditor ultimately accountable to the audit committee. The external audit oversight function (EAOF) of the audit committee includes the following responsibilities: (1) appointment, compensation, and retention of the independent auditors; (2) overseeing the work of the independent auditors; (3) approving all audit and permissible non-audit services; (4) reviewing auditor report on annual financial statements; (5) reviewing auditor report on quarterly financial statements; (6) reviewing auditor report on ICFR; (7) monitoring the external auditors independence; and (8) evaluating independent auditor performance. These responsibilities are examined in the remainder of this chapter.

The Role of External Auditors in Corporate Reporting and Financial Market

Reliability of financial and non-financial information disseminated by public companies to the financial market is vital in maintaining the market safe, efficient, and prosperous as more than 150 million Americans invest in the capital markets. External auditors have common interest and professional obligations to ensure quality and reliability of financial statements and related audits. Management and external auditors have different agenda and responsibilities for financial and audit reports with a common goal of making financial statements free of material misstatements whether caused by errors or by fraud. Financial scandals (e.g., Enron, WorldCom) at the turn of the 21st century and the 2007– 009 global financial crises have eroded investor confidence in public financial information and capital markets and initiatives have taken to restore public trust and investor confidence. Examples of these initiatives are regulatory reforms (e.g., SOX of 2002, SEC rules), corporate governance measures and best practices at corporate level, and accounting and auditing standards by standard-setters (e.g., Financial Accounting Standards Board [FASB], PCAOB). These initiatives while proven to be effective are often not proactive and cost-efficient, and audit firms have not been required by market mechanisms to compete on quality and internally define audit quality and develop a quality control system to effectively measure audit quality and continuously monitor high-quality audit with proper tone at the top in promoting competency, integrity, independence, and audit quality.

The current structure and form of audit practice engagement goes back to the requirements of the Securities Act of 1933 and the Securities Exchange Act of 1934 for the audit of financial statements of public companies by independent private audit firms. SEC regulations have addressed the roles and responsibilities of audit firms in protecting investors from receiving materially misstated audited financial statements. Therefore, it seems reasonable to anticipate that investors' confidence in audited financial information was adversely impacted by perceived lower audit quality that might have persisted in the absence of adequate audit regulations. The auditing profession has a long history of contributing to the effective and efficient function of business operations, the capital markets, and the economy by adding credibility to financial statements. Audit quality and effectiveness and thus the auditor's reputation is the cornerstone of the auditing profession. Narrowing the perceived trust gap and restoring public confidence in financial reports and audit functions will take time and considerable efforts by legislators, regulators, standard-setting bodies, and the accounting profession. The public trust in auditor's judgments plays an important role in accepting audit functions as value-added services, which lend credibility to published financial statements. This trust can be enhanced by auditors focusing on their core values of integrity, objectivity, independence, and competence. Global investor confidence can be improved by strengthening auditor independence and enhancing audit quality.

The Board of Directors and Audit Committee Role in Overseeing External Audit Function

The SOX of 2002 and related SEC implementation rules significantly affect the structure, composition, functions, and responsibilities of the board of directors and its representative the audit committee. Underlying both SOX and the SEC Rules is the presumption that the presence of certain features in the audit committee is a prerequisite for the committee to effectively fulfill its oversight function of the financial and audit process. Specifically, the audit committee should be independent, competent, financially literate, adequately resourced, and properly compensated. This position is underscored by prior research that finds that market participants consider the audit committee as providing vigilant oversight of the financial reporting and audit process.[2] SOX and the SEC-related implementation rules have shifted some of management's financial reporting and audit involvements responsibilities to the audit committee. The board of directors of a company or its audit committee is in charge of hiring auditors and overseeing the responsibilities of the company's management and its auditor. The audit engagement usually is based on the conditions specified in an engagement letter. The conditions of the engagement including audit fee, responsibilities of the management, and the responsibilities of auditors, as well as the market relevance of these conditions should be determined by the audit committee. There should be two-way communication between the company's audit committee and its independent auditor. The audit committee, on one hand, provides the independent auditor with information about the company's corporate governance, its business and industry, the possible strengths and weaknesses in ICFR, the possibility of a business combination, possible wrong doing, or allegations of fraud. The information provided by the audit committee to the independent auditor should assist the auditor in properly planning the integrated audit of financial statements and ICFR, and this improves the quality and effectiveness of the integrated audit.

The audit committee, on the other hand, receives information from the independent auditor regarding the integrated audit of financial statements and ICFR. An effective and candid relationship between the audit committee and the independent auditor can assist in preventing and detecting financial statement fraud. The audit committee can provide the independent auditor information about fraud, risk, business events, transactions, and financial reporting areas that require more audit attention. The independent auditor should inform the audit committee about fraud risks being assessed, audit procedures being applied, and audit findings pertaining to financial statement fraud.[3] The audit committee should evaluate the performance of independent auditors to ensure that the company receives the highest quality audit, and to protect investors from the adverse consequences of poor audit performance and audit failures. In assessing the independent auditor's performance and audit quality, the audit committee should: (1) receive inputs and feedback from management and internal auditors regarding the competence, technical and industry knowledge, professional qualifications, personal integrity, and quality of services provided by the audit engagement team; (2) review the independent auditor's quality control procedures; (3) discuss with the lead partner the overall quality of the audit, the performance of the audit engagement team, and any suggestions or improvements for the integrated audit of both ICFR and audit of financial statements.[4]

In assessing the quality of the audit performed by external auditors, the audit committee should ask the following questions[5]:

1. Did the lead audit partner and audit team have the necessary industry, company, accounting and auditing expertise, knowledge, and skills to meet the company's audit requirements?
2. Were the right resources (manager and senior auditors, staff) dedicated to the audit?
3. Did the auditor seek feedback on the quality of the services provided?
4. Was the lead audit partner accessible to the audit committee and company management?
5. Did the lead audit partner devote sufficient attention and leadership to the audit?
6. Was the review partner engaged in the review of the audit including the planning, conducting, and reporting processes.
7. Did the lead audit partner discuss the audit plan and audit risk (including fraud risk) with the audit committee?
8. Did the lead audit partner discuss any risks of fraud in the financial statement that were factored into the audit plan with the audit committee?
9. Did the lead audit partner perform forensic-related audit procedures to discover alleged financial statement fraud?
10. Did the auditor meet the agreed-upon performance criteria as reflected in the engagement letter and audit plan?
11. Did the auditor advise the audit committee of being subject to inspection by regulators (PCAOB)?

12. Did the auditor communicate the results of the firm's inspection more generally, such as findings regarding companies in similar industries with similar accounting/audit issues that may be pertinent to the company?

13. Did the auditor explain how the firm planned to respond to the inspection findings and to internal findings regarding its quality control program?

14. Was the cost of the audit reasonable and sufficient for the size, complexity, and risks of the company?

15. Did the lead audit partner maintain a professional and open, complete, and frank dialogue with the audit committee and audit committee chair?

16. Was the lead audit partner able to explain accounting and auditing issues in an understandable manner?

17. Did the auditor adequately discuss the quality of the company's financial reporting, including the reasonableness of accounting estimates and judgments?

18. Did the audit firm report to the audit committee all matters that might reasonably be thought to bear on the audit firm's independence, including exceptions to its compliance with independence requirements?

19. Did the audit committee agree with the extent of external auditors' reliance on management and internal audit testing?

20. Were there any significant differences in views between the internal auditors and the auditor and whether and how they were resolved?

21. Did external auditors perform any pre-approved non-audit services and what safeguards were in place to preserve auditors' independence?

Independent Auditors' Role in Improving Audit Quality

The common understanding is that the primary role of auditors is to protect investors from receiving materially misleading financial information by lending credibility to financial statements published by public companies as reflected and measured by audit quality. External auditors can effectively discharge this responsibility by improving audit quality. Audit quality is commonly perceived as auditor's ability to discover material misstatements in the audited financial statements and willingness to report discovered material misstatements. However, audit quality is difficult to measure mainly because there is a lack of a commonly accepted definition. DeAngelo (1981) defines audit quality as "the market assessed joint probability that a given auditor will both discover a breach in a client's accounting system, and report the breach".[6] The role of auditors and the value relevance of audit report have recently been challenged. The 2010 inspection reports of the PCAOB suggest that auditors failed to fulfill their gatekeeping responsibility of protecting investors from receiving misleading financial reports by: (1) not challenging the assumptions of valuation models; (2) allowing inadequate risk assessment of off-balance sheet transactions; and (3) not providing early signal of financial difficulties and inability to continue as going concern.[7]

Audit failure occurs when a company with reported unqualified financial statements discloses low-quality and misleading financial information or has to restate previously audited financial statements. One of the lessons auditors should learn from the recent audit failures is to exercise great due professional care in deciding whether to waive or report discovered misstatements. The public trust in auditor's judgments plays an important role in accepting audit functions as value-added services, which lend credibility to published financial statements. This trust can be enhanced by auditors focusing on their core values of integrity, objectivity, independence, and competence. Global investor confidence can be improved by strengthening auditor independence and enhancing audit quality.

How to Improve Audit Quality

The PCAOB has initially developed an audit quality framework that is based on past studies and current standards consisting of three segments: audit inputs, processes, and results.[8] The PCAOB creates audit quality indicators to "measure elements of the audit quality framework, which in turn provide insight into audit quality."[9] The audit quality framework suggested in the 2015 PCAOB Concept Release contributes to a clearer view of auditing by identifying key variables, or indicators, to inform discussions about audit quality.[10] The three principles underlying the development of the framework is that they be quantitative if possible, generate usable data to pose critical questions, and they be used as a "balanced portfolio" of audit quality to reflect how the indicators work collectively. The heart of the framework is to identify indicators that can signal quality in the conduct of an audit.

The PCAOB has identified 28 potential indicators classified under three main categories: audit professionals (inputs), audit process (processes), and audit results (outputs). These categories have sub-categories. Audit professionals concern availability, competence, and focus indicators. The audit process category includes tone at the top and leadership, incentives, independence, infrastructure, and monitoring and remediation indicators. Finally, the audit results category includes financial statements, internal control, going concern, communications between auditors and audit committees, and enforcement and litigation indicators. Similar audit quality framework is developed by the International Auditing and Assurance Standards Board (IAASB) in February 2014, entitled "A Framework for Audit Quality."[11] The stated objectives of the IAASB framework on audit quality (AQ) are to address the key elements of AQ, facilitate dialogue between users of AQ to find ways to improve AQ (IAASB, 2014). The IAASB framework consists of five components of input factors, process factors, output factors, key indicators, and conceptual factors.[12]

Audit quality, as well as the relevancy of the audit, can be improved by the following: (1) implementing an expanded audit report; (2) requiring the signature or identification of the engagement partner; (3) implementing a rebuttable presumption that abnormally low audit fees will result in inspection; (4) requiring independent directors on firm governing and advisory boards; (5) heightening auditor going-concern reporting; and (6) allowing shareholder proposals on auditor issues. Implementing an expanded audit report will improve audit quality by allowing the auditor to highlight specific client accounting that is pushing the bounds of acceptability. First, the expanded report will include meaningful and incremental information that is more relevant for both investment and stewardship purposes. Second, requiring identification of the engagement partner will make that partner more diligent and cautious when working on audits. Third, implementing a presumption that results in inspection of audits with low fees will result in an improvement of audit quality. Research finds that there is a strong positive relation between fees and hours, and thus, audit quality. Fourth, audit quality can be improved by enhancing audit firm governance by requiring independent directors on firm governing and advisory boards.

Independent directors will be an advocate for the public interest and will act as a disciplining mechanism on firm decisions and actions. Fifth, audit quality can be improved by heightening auditor going-concern reporting. Audit quality will improve if investors are provided with an early warning of an impending firm failure. Finally, allowing shareholder proposals on auditing issues will improve audit quality by more closely aligning the auditor's incentives with those of users of the audit services.

PCAOB Initiatives

The PCAOB recent initiatives in improving audit quality among others include[13]:

- Analysis of Audits Affected by the Economic Crisis—The examination of audit deficiencies that inspectors uncovered in inspections during the period 2007 through 2009.
- Root Cause Analysis—Identification of the root causes of audit deficiencies and actions needed to mitigate the identified audit deficiencies.
- Correction of Past Deficiencies—Implementation of adequate and effective audit quality control policies and procedures to prevent further occurrences of identified audit deficiencies to protect investors and to rebuild public trust and investor confidence in financial statement audits.
- Firm Management and Monitoring—Proper examination of audit firms' management and monitoring process (appropriate tone at the top) by determining whether the supervision and monitoring systems are effective in detecting and preventing audit failures.
- Strengthening Auditor Independence—Complying with auditor independence requirements, and implementing performance review processes to ensure audit effectiveness.
- Audit quality Indicators Concept Release

These initiatives taken by the PCAOB are intended to improve audit quality worldwide including the supervision of Cross-border Audits of

Multi-location Companies and investigation of the quality control system of international audit firms in the global networks that audit multinational corporations. The PCAOB evaluates the quality of cooperation, communication, and coordination among affiliates in these audit firms' networks. Narrowing the perceived trust gap and restoring public confidence in financial reports and audit functions will take time and considerable efforts by legislators, regulators, standard-setting bodies, and the accounting profession.

Audit Committee Oversight of External Auditors

External auditors play a vital role in the financial reporting process. As a result, effective oversight of auditors is at the core of the audit committee's responsibilities. For all U. S. public companies, the audit committee is "directly responsible for the appointment, compensation, and oversight" of the external auditor. Extensive laws and regulations, including SOX requirements, SEC rules, auditing standards, and stock exchange listing rules, govern the audit committee's relationship with the external auditor. In general, the audit committee's oversight standards are as follows:

- Appointment, retention, evaluation, and compensation of the external auditor.
- Monitoring the external auditor's independence, including rotation of the audit partners and preapproval of audit and non-audit services, which are strictly limited under SEC regulations and therefore require a clear preapproval policy and process.
- Overseeing the auditor's interim review procedures.
- Overseeing the strategy, scope, progress, and results of the external audit of financial statements and audit of ICOFR.

There are some suggested practices that can help the audit committee carry out its oversight responsibilities and build a strong relationship with the external auditor. First, a strong working relationship should be built between the audit committee chair and the lead audit engagement partner. A strong working relationship is essential to the audit committees and the engagement team's effectiveness. This relationship between the chair and the audit partner lays the foundation for productive communications between the engagement team and the audit committee as a whole. Second, the audit committee should develop a clear plan for audit partner rotations, as well as rotations for key members of the engagement team. Lead audit engagement partners must be rotated every five years. To avoid disruptions, committees should ensure that the audit firm has a clear schedule and timeline for partner rotations, as well as a process to identify new partners to assume these positions. Lastly, audit committees need to consider how they can most effectively carry out its "direct responsibility" for oversight of the external auditor given management's extensive interactions with the engagement team. This can be related to areas such as evaluating the auditor's performance, partner rotation, and reviewing audit plans. In these areas, management works closely with the engagement team, and definitely has important insights and knowledge that can help the audit committee carry out its responsibility, but in all these areas the audit committee has the final responsibility.

Audit Firm Selection and Ratification

Section 301 of SOX makes the audit committee of each public company "directly responsible" for the appointment, compensation, and oversight of the work of any registered accounting firm employed by the issuer to prepare or issue an audit. In selecting an independent auditor, audit committees consider a number of factors including: (1) the quality of its ongoing discussions with the independent auditor, including the professional resolution of accounting and financial reporting matters with the national office; (2) the professional qualifications of the lead audit partner and other key engagement partners; (3) the independent auditor's independence program and its processes for maintaining its independence; (4) the auditor's depth of understanding of the company's global businesses, accounting policies, and practices, and ICFR; (5) the appropriateness of the auditor's fees for both audit and non-audit services; (6) the most recent PCAOB inspection report on the independent auditor; (7) the results of management's and the audit committee's annual evaluations of the qualifications, performances, and independence of the independent auditor; and (8) the auditor's expertise and capabilities in handling the complexity of the company's businesses.

Audit Firm Compensation

The SOX of 2002 requires that the audit committee have authority and adequate funding to compensate independent auditors for approved and performed audit and non-audit services. When performing any audit or permissible non-audit service, independent auditors must report directly to the audit committee. The company must provide appropriate funding to the accounting firm as determined by the audit committee. The independent auditor's compensation should include fees for: (1) audit of annual financial statements; (2) audit of ICFR; (3) review of quarterly financial statements; and (4) performance of permissible non-audit services.

The Center of Audit Quality (2015) reviewed additional auditor compensation disclosures to determine whether more audit committees are explicitly stating the role they play in determining the audit firm's compensation.[14] Disclosure that the audit committee is responsible for audit firm compensation doubled from the prior year among S&P 500 companies. Audit committees are making a concerted effort to share with investors the direct and primary role they play in determining audit firm compensation both in the ratification of the appointment of the audit firm section of the proxy and the audit committee report.

Selection of Audit Partner

Alongside enhanced disclosure around factors considered in selecting an audit firm, there was also more robust discussion around the role the audit committee plays in engagement partner selection, as well as a statement that the engagement partner rotates every five years. This was particularly evident among this year's S&P 500 proxies.[15] In accordance with SEC rules and policies, audit partners are subject to rotation requirements to limit the number of consecutive years an individual partner may provide service to a company. For lead and concurring audit partners, the maximum number of consecutive years of service in that capacity is five years. A company will select the company's lead audit partner pursuant to this rotation policy following meetings between the Chairman of the Audit Committee and candidates for that role, as well as discussion by the full Committee and with management.

Review of Annual Audited Financial Statements

In the United States, the financial statement audit of public companies is performed by the registered independent auditor in accordance with the auditing standards of the Public Company Accounting Oversight Board in the Unites States.[16] Independent auditors use their judgment in deciding about audit planning and scope of evidence-gathering procedures. Nevertheless, the audit committee should obtain sufficient understanding of audit plans and the scope of audits. Independent auditors should discuss their audit plans and scope with the audit committee to ensure that the audit covers all areas identified in the engagement letter (a written contract) to identify areas of high financial risk (e.g., related-party transactions). Independent auditors should also inform the audit committee of any significant changes in audit plan and scope throughout the audit of financial statements.

The audit committee should directly receive the draft audit report, review the audit report, and after careful review submit it to the board of directors. Exhibit 3.1 shows the standard unqualified report of the independent registered accounting firm according to PCAOB Auditing Standard No. 1. Exhibit 3.2 presents GE's audit report on its 2014 financial statements based on the integrated approach suggested by the PCAOB.

The audit committee should review the draft audit report by meeting separately with the independent auditor and management. In meeting with the independent auditor, the audit committee should ascertain that: (1) the audit was conducted according to the initially discussed audit plan and scope, any significant changes in the audit plan or scope, the company's critical accounting policies and procedures; (2) the independent auditor and management have discussed all alternative treatments within generally accepted accounting principles (GAAP) for policies and practices, any significant deficiencies and material weaknesses in the ICFR identified by the independent auditors, the audit findings, conclusions, opinion, and the extent of management cooperation with the independent auditor; and (3) appropriate responses have been initialed to address any material fraud and significant illegal act, violation of securities laws discovered by the independent auditor. In meeting separately with management, the audit committee should discuss: (1) the quality

Exhibit 3.1

Report of independent registered public accounting firm

We have audited the accompanying balance sheets of X Company as of December 31, 20X3 and 20X2, and the related statements of operations, stockholders' equity, and cash flows for each of the three years in the period ended December 31, 20X3. These financial statements are the responsibility of the Company's management. Our responsibility is to express an opinion on these financial statements based on our audits.

We conducted our audits in accordance with the standards of the Public Company Accounting Oversight Board (United States). Those standards require that we plan and perform the audit to obtain reasonable assurance about whether the financial statements are free of material misstatement. An audit includes examining, on a test basis, evidence supporting the amounts and disclosures in the financial statements. An audit also includes assessing the accounting principles used and significant estimates made by management, as well as evaluating the overall financial statement presentation. We believe that our audits provide a reasonable basis for our opinion.

In our opinion, the financial statements referred to above present fairly, in all material respects, the financial position of the Company as of [at] December 31, 20X3 and 20X2, and the results of its operations and its cash flows for each of the three years in the period ended December 31, 20X3, in conformity with U.S. generally accepted accounting principles.

[*Signature*]

[City and State or Country]

[*Date*]

Source: adapted from the Public Company Accounting Oversight Board. Available at: www. pcaobus.org

of the performance of the independent auditor, and (2) management's assessment of the independent auditor's understanding of the company's internal control, business operations, industry practices, financial risks, and other significant accounting policies and practices.

Approving Audit and Non-Audit Services

Section 202 of SOX generally requires a public company's audit committee to pre-approve all auditing services and non-audit services provided to the

Exhibit 3.2

Report of independent registered public accounting firm

To Shareowners and board of directors of General Electric Company:

We have audited the accompanying statement of financial position of General Electric Company and consolidated affiliates (the "Company") as of December 31, 2014 and 2013, and the related statements of earnings, comprehensive income, changes in shareowners' equity, and cash flows for each of the years in the three-year period ended December 31, 2014. We also have audited the Company's internal control over financial reporting (ICFR) as of December 31, 2014, based on criteria established in Internal Control ± Integrated Framework (2013) issued by the Committee of Sponsoring Organizations of the Treadway Commission (COSO). The company's management is responsible for these consolidated financial statements, for maintaining effective ICFR, and for its assessment of the effectiveness of ICFR. Our responsibility is to express an opinion on these consolidated financial statements and an opinion on the Company's ICFR based on our audits.

We conducted our audits in accordance with the standards of the Public Company Accounting Oversight Board (United States). Those standards require that we plan and perform the audits to obtain reasonable assurance about whether the financial statements are free of material misstatement and whether effective ICFR was maintained in all material respects. Our audits of the consolidated financial statements included examining, on a test basis, evidence supporting the amounts and disclosures in the financial statements, assessing the accounting principles used and significant estimates made by management, and evaluating the overall financial statement presentation. Our audit of ICFR included obtaining an understanding of ICFR, assessing the risk that a material weakness exists, and testing and evaluating the design and operating effectiveness of internal control based on the assessed

(Continued)

Exhibit 3.2 (*Continued*)

risk. Our audits also included performing such other procedures as we considered necessary in the circumstances. We believe that our audits provide a reasonable basis for our opinions.

A company's ICFR is a process designed to provide reasonable assurance regarding the reliability of financial reporting and the preparation of financial statements for external purposes in accordance with GAAP. A company's ICFR includes those policies and procedures that: (1) pertain to the maintenance of records that, in reasonable detail, accurately and fairly reflect the transactions and dispositions of the assets of the company; (2) provide reasonable assurance that transactions are recorded as necessary to permit preparation of financial statements in accordance with generally accepted accounting principles, and that receipts and expenditures of the company are being made only in accordance with authorizations of management and directors of the company; and (3) provide reasonable assurance regarding prevention or timely detection of unauthorized acquisition, use, or disposition of the company's assets that could have a material effect on the financial statements. Because of its inherent limitations, ICFR may not prevent or detect misstatements. Also, projections of any evaluation of effectiveness to future periods are subject to the risk that controls may become inadequate because of changes in conditions, or that the degree of compliance with the policies or procedures may deteriorate.

In our opinion, the consolidated financial statements present fairly, in all material respects, the financial position of General Electric Company and consolidated affiliates as of December 31, 2014 and 2013, and the results of their operations and their cash flows for each of the years in the three-year period ended December 31, 2014, in conformity with U.S. generally accepted accounting principles. Also in our opinion, the Company maintained, in all material respects, effective ICFR as of December 31, 2014, based on criteria established in Internal Control $\pm$ Integrated Framework (2013) issued by COSO.

Our audits of the consolidated financial statements were made for the purpose of forming an opinion on the consolidated financial statements taken as a whole. The accompanying consolidating information

appearing on pages 129, 133, and 135 is presented for purposes of additional analysis of the consolidated financial statements rather than to
present the financial position, results of operations, and cash flows of the
individual entities. The consolidating information has been subjected to
the auditing procedures applied in the audits of the consolidated financial statements and, in our opinion, is fairly stated in all material respects
in relation to the consolidated financial statements taken as a whole.

/s/ KPMG LLP

KPMG LLP

Stamford, Connecticut

February 27, 2015

Source: Adapted from GE's Proxy Statement and 10-K Report filed with the SEC. Available
at: www.ge.com/ar2014/assets/pdf/GE_AR14.pdf

company. Section 201 of the Act and SEC rules classify services often performed by independent auditors as: (1) audit; (2) audit-related; (3) tax;
and (4) other non-audit services.[17]

An accounting firm auditing a public company may not
contemporaneously provide the company the following non-audit services:
bookkeeping, financial information system design and implementation,
actuarial services, appraisal, valuation services, internal audit outsourc-
ing, management function, broker-dealer and investment advising, legal
services, expert witness services.[18] The audit committee must pre-approve
all other permitted non-audit services including tax services. Under rules
that the PCAOB has adopted pending their approval by the SEC, an
independent auditor could not perform for an audit client three types
of tax services: (1) services under contingent fee arrangements (e.g., tax
shelter fees based on the percentage of tax savings); (2) services related to
the planning or opinion of the tax consequences of a transaction that is
listed as an aggressive transaction under Treasury regulations, or is based
on an aggressive interpretation of applicable tax laws and regulations (tax
shelters); and (3) tax services to senior executive officers in the financial
reporting oversight role (selling of tax services to senior officers).[19]

The audit committee should approve all audit and permissible
non-audit services to be provided by the registered auditor. Under SEC

rules, the pre-approval process should be established by the company and may take place in several ways[20]:

- The audit committee pre-approves audit services and permissible non-audit service on a case-by-case basis; or
- The company establishes general pre-approval policies and procedures under the oversight responsibility of the audit committee provided that: (1) the established pre-approval policies and procedures are itemized by type of service; (2) these policies and procedures do not include delegating pre-approval responsibilities of the audit committee to management; and (3) the audit committee is informed of each service to be performed by the independent auditors.
- The audit committee may delegate the pre-approval responsibility to an audit committee member(s) provided the delegated member's decisions are reported to the entire audit committee in subsequent meetings.
- The company may use a combination of the above options.

SOX and SEC rules include *minims* exceptions (for minor amounts of services) for: (1) non-audit services, which in the aggregate are not greater than five percent of the total annual fees paid to the independent auditor for all services (audit and permissible non-audit); (2) such services were not initially recognized by the company as non-audit services at the time of the engagement; (3) such services are promptly brought to the attention of the company's audit committee and subsequently approved by the audit committee or a designated member of the audit committee prior to the completion of the audit engagement; and (4) such services and their subsequent approvals are properly disclosed to investors through the company's annual report and the annual meeting proxy statement. The audit committee should also establish an annual budget for each category of audit and permissible non-audit services to be performed by the independent auditor. These rules are designed to ensure that the audit firm remains truly independent of the audit client and its management. Throughout an audit engagement, the audit committee should monitor auditor independence to ensure that auditors maintain their independence according to applicable laws, regulations, and standards throughout the audit engagement. The Deloitte & Touche 2003 survey reveals that about 70 percent of respondents reported that they have already adopted policies and procedures for pre-approval requirements and the other 30 percent are in the process of establishing such policies and procedures.[21]

Communication between Audit Committee and Independent Auditor

There should be two-way communication between the company's audit committee and its independent auditor. The audit committee, on one hand, provides the independent auditor with information about the company's corporate governance, its business and industry, the possible strengths and weaknesses in ICFR, the possibility of a business combination, possible wrong doing, or allegations of fraud. The information provided by the audit committee to the independent auditor should assist the auditor in properly planning the integrated audit of financial statements and ICFR and this improves the quality and effectiveness of the integrated audit.

The audit committee, on the other hand, receives information from the independent auditor regarding the integrated audit of financial statements and ICFR. Information the audit committee receives from the independent auditor according to Statement of Auditing Standard (SAS) No. 61, SAS No. 90, and PCAOB Auditing Standards (AS) No. 2 include the following.[22]

1. The responsibility assumed by the independent auditor in an integrated audit of financial statements and ICFR.
2. Significant accounting policies and practices and changes in accounting principles.
3. The basis for management judgments and methods used to develop accounting estimates, accruals, and reserves.
4. The effect of proposed significant audit adjustments on financial statements.

5. The responsibility assumed by the independent auditor for other information in documents containing audited financial statements.
6. Any significant disagreements with management regarding financial reports and internal controls.
7. Consultation with other auditor on auditing and accounting matters.
8. Any discussion of allegations of fraud.
9. Significant deficiencies and material weaknesses in ICFR.
10. Management discussion with the independent auditor about the quality, not just the acceptability, of the company's accounting principles and underlying estimates in the financial statements.
11. The independent auditor rotation requirements.
12. Disclosure of total auditor fees and breakdowns into audit fees, audit-related fees, tax service fees, and the aggregated amount of other fees.
13. Compliance with pre-approval policies and procedures for audit and permissible non-audit services.
14. Disclosures about auditor independence.

An effective and candid relationship between the audit committee and the independent auditor can assist in preventing and detecting financial statement fraud. The audit committee can provide the independent auditor information about fraud, risk, business events, transactions, and financial reporting areas that require more audit attention. The independent auditor should inform the audit committee about fraud risks being assessed, and audit procedures being applied, and audit findings pertaining to financial statement fraud.

Internal Control Over Financial Reporting

Many provisions of SOX pertain to financial reporting including Sections 302 and 404 that require public companies' management to certify financial statements and report on the effectiveness of the company's ICFR and require auditors to attest to and report on both financial statements and ICFR. Section 301 requires that the audit committee oversees the work of management and the independent auditor as related to ICFR. The audit committee's oversight of Section 404 is essential as mandatory ICFR is becoming an integral part of financial reporting. SOX provisions directed the SEC to issue rules and Interpretive Guidance and the PCAOB to issue Auditing Standards (AS) No. 2 and 5 in requiring the use of the Integrated Financial and Internal Control Reporting (IFICR) concept.[23] Section 404 of SOX requires the independent auditor to attest to and report on management's assessment of the company's ICFR and directs the PCAOB to issue guidance on the auditor report on internal control.[24] PCAOB Auditing Standards Nos. 2 and 5, An Audit of Internal Control over Financial Reporting Performance in Conjunctions with an Audit of Financial Statements (AS Nos. 2 &5), establishes guidance for the audit of ICFR.[25] AS No. 5 is intended to improve the audit by: (1) focusing the audit on the matters most important to internal control; (2) eliminating unnecessary audit procedures; (3) simplifying the auditor requirements; and (4) scaling the integrated audit for smaller companies.

The effectiveness of ICFR depends on the vigilant oversight function of the board of directors, particularly the audit committee, the responsible and accountable managerial function of senior executives, the credible external audit function of the independent auditor, and the objective internal audit function of internal auditors. In expressing an opinion on ICFR, the independent auditor must perform tests of controls to evaluate: (1) management's assessment of the effectiveness of ICFR by gathering sufficient competent evidence about both the process used and the conclusion reached by management; and (2) the effectiveness of both the design and operation of ICFR. Any deficiencies found in ICFR must be evaluated in terms of their possible effects on misstatements of an account balance or disclosure.

To facilitate the move toward cost-effective IFICR, the SEC and the PCAOB have taken several initiatives in recent years. The SEC issued interpretive guidance for management's assessment of the effectiveness of ICFR. The PCAOB revised its auditing standards, particularly AS No. 5, for audits of ICFR. These initiatives have made Section 404 of SOX on internal control compliance more cost-effective, efficient, and scalable and provided a framework for effective implementation of IFICR. SEC Interpretive Guidance provides guidance for the effective implementation of Section 404 of SOX in the following six key areas: (1) management must

assess the effectiveness of the company's ICFR; (2) the independent auditor must opine only on the effectiveness of ICFR, not management's assessment; (3) the focus of the internal control audit should be on the most
important matters that present the greatest risk that a company's internal
controls will fail to detect, prevent, or correct material misstatements in
its financial statements by using a top-down, risk-based approach of focusing on company-level controls and its control environment; (4) unnecessary audit procedures should be eliminated to achieve the intended
benefits of the audit by using the experience gained in previous years'
audits and from the work of others (e.g., internal auditors, management)
and focusing on the assessment of the opinion on the effectiveness of
internal controls rather than adequacy of management's process to reach
its conclusion; (5) the integrated audit should be scaled to fit the size and
complexity of the company, particularly making the auditing standards
more scalable for smaller companies; and (6) auditing standards should
be simplified by making them shorter, more transparent, and more clearly
scalable to audits of companies of all sizes.

PCAOB AS No. 5, along with the SEC's Interpretive Guidance for
management, is expected to substantially reduce the total cost of compliance with Section 404. The extent of cost savings depends on a variety of
factors and may vary from company to company, including the extent to
which both management and auditors have previously implemented a risk-
based and top-down approach in their assessment and audit of ICFR. AS
No. 5 is designed to be scalable to the size and complexity of a company by
allowing the auditor to align the level of audit effort and evidence-gathering
procedures with the assessed level of risk and complexity. Thus, AS No. 5
properly directs auditors to scale the audit and provide sufficient guidance
for auditors in applying the scaling concept. AS No. 5 is intended to focus
audit attention on the matters most important to internal control, elimi-
nate unnecessary procedures, simplify auditing requirements, and scale the
audit for companies of varying sizes and complexities.

Auditing standards (AS Nos. 2 and 5) issued by the PCAOB recommend
the use of an integrated audit approach consisting of an audit of ICFR and
the financial statements. The integrated audit requires independent auditors to express an opinion on: management's assessment of the effectiveness of ICFR; the effectiveness of both the design and operation of ICFR;

and the fair presentation of financial statements in conformity with GAAP. The phrase "integrated audit" appeared for the first time in the title of professional standards when the PCAOB issued its AS No. 5.[26] PCAOB AS No. 5 supersedes AS No. 2 and was developed in response to the perceived ineffectiveness, inefficiency, and lack of scalability of AS No. 2 and in an attempt to encourage auditors to use a principles-based, top-down, risk-based audit, and to apply professional judgment to tailor the integrated audit to the facts and circumstances of each audit engagement. AS No. 5 is intended to improve the audit quality by: (1) focusing the audit on the matters most important to internal control; (2) eliminating unnecessary audit procedures; (3) simplifying the auditor requirements; and (4) scaling the integrated audit for smaller companies.

Circumstances Possibly Indicating Material Weaknesses

PCAOB auditing standards (AS Nos. 2 and 5) provide a list of circumstances that may result in a significant deficiency indicating that a material weakness in ICFR exists. These circumstances include the following[27]:

1. Restatement of previously issued financial statements reflecting the correction of a misstatement.
2. Identification of a material misstatement in the current period financial statements that were undetected by the company's ICFR.
3. Ineffective oversight functions of the company's audit committee regarding its financial reporting and ICFR.
4. Ineffective internal control or risk assessment function to monitor the company's risk assessment related to complex business events or transaction.
5. Ineffective regulatory compliance function to ensure compliance with applicable laws and regulations particularly for complex companies in highly regulated industries.
6. Identification of any financial statement fraud.
7. Uncorrected significant deficiencies that were previously communicated to the company's management and the audit committee by the independent auditor and remain uncorrected after some reasonable period of time.

8. An ineffective control environment that creates opportunities for the occurrence of significant deficiencies or material weaknesses in the company's ICFR.

Classification of Internal Control Deficiencies

PCAOB auditing standards (AS Nos. 2 and 5) state that when internal control deficiencies are identified, they should be classified into the following three categories[28]:

1. Inconsequential Deficiencies: These are internal control deficiencies that either are not material or do not have significant adversarial effects on fair presentation of financial statements in conforming with GAAP.
2. Significant Deficiencies: Significant deficiencies are either significant internal control deficiencies or a combination of internal control deficiencies that cause ICFR to not be effective in preventing or detecting misstatements that are more than inconsequential in the annual or interim financial statements. These significant control deficiencies adversely affect the company's ability to initiate, measure, authorize, recognize, process, and report financial information in accordance with GAAP. These significant deficiencies can occur either in the design and/or the operation of the ICFR.
3. Material Weakness: Material weaknesses are either a significant control deficiency, or a combination of significant deficiencies that result in more than a remote likelihood that a material misstatement in financial statements (annual or interim) will not be prevented or detected. That is, it is probable or reasonably possible that a company's ICFR is not effective in preventing and detecting material misstatements in financial reports.

The Independent Auditor's Report

The independent audit report on ICFR can be a separate report or combined with the audit report on the financial statements. Exhibit 3.3 shows the format and content of both a separate audit report on

Exhibit 3.3

Report of independent registered public accounting firm

[Introductory paragraph]

We have audited management's assessment, included in the accompanying *[title of management's report]*, that W Company maintained effective internal control over financial reporting as of December 31, 20X3, based on *[Identify control criteria, for example, "criteria established in Internal Control—Integrated Framework issued by the Committee of Sponsoring Organizations of the Treadway Commission (COSO).]*. W Company's management is responsible for maintaining effective internal control over financial reporting and for its assessment of the effectiveness of internal control over financial reporting. Our responsibility is to express an opinion on management's assessment and an opinion on the effectiveness of the company's internal control over financial reporting based on our audit.

[Scope paragraph]

We conducted our audit in accordance with the standards of the Public Company Accounting Oversight Board (United States). Those standards require that we plan and perform the audit to obtain reasonable assurance about whether effective internal control over financial reporting was maintained in all material respects. Our audit included obtaining an understanding of internal control over financial reporting, evaluating management's assessment, testing and evaluating the design and operating effectiveness of internal control, and performing such other procedures as we

[Definition paragraph]

A company's internal control over financial reporting is a process designed to provide reasonable assurance regarding the reliability of financial reporting and the preparation of financial statements for external purposes in accordance with generally accepted accounting principles. A company's internal control over financial reporting includes those policies and procedures that (1) pertain to the maintenance of records that, in reasonable detail, accurately and fairly reflect the transactions and dispositions of the assets of the company; (2) provide reasonable assurance that transactions are recorded as necessary to permit preparation of financial statements in accordance with generally accepted accounting principles, and that receipts and expenditures of the company are being made only in accordance with authorizations of management and directors of the company; and (3) provide reasonable assurance regarding prevention or timely detection of unauthorized acquisition, use, or disposition of the company's assets that could have a material effect on the financial statements.

[Inherent limitations paragraph]

Because of its inherent limitations, internal control over financial reporting may not prevent or detect misstatements. Also, projections of any evaluation of effectiveness to future periods are subject to the risk that controls may become inadequate because of changes in conditions, or that the degree of compliance with the policies or procedures may deteriorate.

(Continued)

Exhibit 3.3 (Continued)

[Opinion paragraph]

In our opinion, management's assessment that W Company maintained effective internal control over financial reporting as of December 31, 20X3, is fairly stated, in all material respects, based on [Identify control criteria, for example, "criteria established in Internal Control—Integrated Framework issued by the Committee of Sponsoring Organizations of the Treadway Commission (COSO)."]. Also in our opinion, W Company maintained, in all material respects, effective internal control over financial reporting as of December 31, 20X3, based on [Identify control criteria, for example,

"criteria established in Internal Control—Integrated Framework issued by the Committee of Sponsoring Organizations of the Treadway Commission (COSO)."].

[Explanatory paragraph]

We have also audited, in accordance with the standards of the Public Company Accounting Oversight Board (United States), the [identify financial statements] of W Company and our report dated [date of report, which should be the same as the date of the report on the effectiveness of internal control over financial reporting] expressed [include nature of opinion].

[Signature]

[City and State or Country]

[Date]

Source: adapted from the Public Company Accounting Oversight Board. Available at: www. pcaobus.org

internal control and a combined report of both financial statements audit and internal control audit. Exhibit 3.2 shows GE's audit report from 2014 in the combined format. Exhibit 3.4 shows the independent auditor report on GM's ICFR in 2014. It is expected that the auditing profession eventually will move toward an integrated audit approach, which is the combined audit of both ICFR and financial statements. An integrated audit approach necessitates the use of an integrated audit report. The author suggests that an integrated audit report be issued particularly when the independent auditor issues an unqualified opinion on both financial statements and ICFR. Nevertheless, management's report on internal control should be a separate report and should be placed right after the management's discussion and analysis (MD&A) section of Form 10-K and immediately before the financial statements section.

Exhibit 3.4

Report of independent registered public accounting firm

General Motors Corporation, its directors, and stockholders:

We have audited the internal control over financial reporting of General Motors Company and subsidiaries (the Company) as of December 31, 2014, based on the criteria established in Internal Control — Integrated Framework (2013) issued by the Committee of Sponsoring Organizations of the Treadway Commission. The Company's management is responsible for maintaining effective internal control over financial reporting and for its assessment of the effectiveness of internal control over financial reporting, included in the accompanying Management's Report on Internal Control over Financial Reporting. Our responsibility is to express an opinion on the Company's internal control over financial reporting based on our audit.

We conducted our audit in accordance with the standards of the Public Company Accounting Oversight Board (United States). Those standards require that we plan and perform the audit to obtain reasonable assurance about whether effective internal control over financial reporting was maintained in all material respects. Our audit included obtaining an understanding of internal control over financial reporting, assessing the risk that a material weakness exists, testing and evaluating the design and operating effectiveness of internal control based on the assessed risk, and performing such other procedures as we considered necessary in the circumstances. We believe that our audit provides a reasonable basis for our opinion.

A company's internal control over financial reporting is a process designed by, or under the supervision of, the company's principal executive and principal financial officers, or persons performing similar functions, and effected by the company's board of directors, management, and other personnel to provide reasonable assurance regarding the reliability of financial reporting and the preparation of financial statements for external purposes in accordance with generally accepted accounting principles. A company's internal control over financial-reporting includes those policies and procedures that (1) pertain to

(*Continued*)

Exhibit 3.4 (*Continued*)

the maintenance of records that, in reasonable detail, accurately and fairly reflect the transactions and dispositions of the assets of the company; (2) provide reasonable assurance that transactions are recorded as necessary to permit preparation of financial statements in accordance with generally accepted accounting principles, and that receipts and expenditures of the company are being made only in accordance with authorizations of management and directors of the company; and (3) provide reasonable assurance regarding prevention or timely detection of unauthorized acquisition, use, or disposition of the company's assets that could have a material effect on the financial statements.

Because of the inherent limitations of internal control over financial reporting, including the possibility of collusion or improper management override of controls, material misstatements due to error or fraud may not be prevented or detected on a timely basis. Also, projections of any evaluation of the effectiveness of the internal control over financial reporting to future periods are subject to the risk that the controls may become inadequate because of changes in conditions, or that the degree of compliance with the policies or procedures may deteriorate.

In our opinion, the Company maintained, in all material respects, effective internal control over financial reporting as of December 31, 2014, based on the criteria established in Internal Control — Integrated Framework (2013) issued by the Committee of Sponsoring Organizations of the Treadway Commission.

We have also audited, in accordance with the standards of the Public Company Accounting Oversight Board (United States), the consolidated financial statements as of and for the year ended December 31, 2014 of the Company and our report dated February 4, 2015 expressed an unqualified opinion on those financial statements.

Deloitte & Touche LLP

Detroit, Michigan

February 4, 2015

Source: Adapted from GM's Proxy Statement and 10-K Report filed with the SEC. Available at: www.gm.com/content/dam/gmcom/COMPANY/Investors/Stockholder_Information/PDFs/2014_GM_Annual_Report.pdf

An auditor's report may express three possible types of audit opinions on ICFR.[29] These options are:

1. Unqualified opinion: The unqualified opinion can be rendered when there are no identified material weaknesses in ICFR and no scope limitations. In this case the audit report states that "In our opinion, management's assessment of the effectiveness of the company's ICFR is fairly stated."

2. Adverse Opinion: The adverse opinion should be rendered when there are significant deficiencies in the company's ICFR that result in one or more material weaknesses. In this case the audit report states that, "In our opinion, management's assessment of the effectiveness of the company's ICFR is not fairly stated."

3. Qualified/Disclaimer Opinion: The disclaimer of opinion should be given when there is a scope limitation and the auditor cannot express an opinion on management's assessment of the effectiveness of the company's ICFR.

PCAOB auditing standards (AS Nos. 2 and 5) state some circumstances where management may conclude that the company's ICFR is ineffective. If the auditor concurs with management's assessment, then the auditor may issue an unqualified opinion on management's assessment and render an adverse opinion on the effectiveness of ICFR. There may be situations where management reports that the company's internal control is effective but the independent auditor discovers material weaknesses that were not corrected and issues an adverse opinion on the effectiveness of the company's ICFR. This could only happen under rare circumstances where there is a strong disagreement between management and the independent auditor regarding the company's ICFR and the audit committee is unable to resolve this disagreement. In these circumstances, the audit committee should work closely with both management and the independent auditor to examine disagreements and try to resolve them in such a way that investors receive relevant and transparent financial information.

The responsibilities that SOX imposes on management and independent auditors for ICFR requires that: (1) management design and maintain internal controls; (2) management document the design and operation of ICFR; (3) management assess the effectiveness of both the design and operation of the company's ICFR; (4) management prepares its report on a timely basis; (5) the audit committee review management's assessment of the effectiveness of ICFR; (6) the independent auditor test controls to gather sufficient competence evidence in evaluating both management's assessment of the effectiveness of ICFR and internal control itself; (7) the independent auditor issues the report on the company's internal over financial reporting on a timely basis, and (8) the audit committee review the independent auditor's report on ICFR. All of the above eight requirements should be met in order for the company to successfully comply with Section 404 of SOX. The audit committee should work with both management and the independent auditor to ensure that these requirements were met and the company is in compliance with Section 404 of the SOX of 2002.

Evaluation of Independent Auditor Performance

The audit committee should evaluate the performance of independent auditors to ensure that the company receives the best quality audit and to protect investors from the adverse consequences of poor audit performance and audit failures. In assessing the independent auditor's performance, the audit committee should: (1) receive inputs and feedback from management and internal auditors regarding the competence, technical and industry knowledge, professional qualifications, personal integrity, and quality of services provided by the audit engagement team; (2) review the independent auditor's quality control procedures; (3) discuss with the lead partner the overall quality of the audit, the performance of the audit engagement team, and any suggestions or improvements for the integrated audit of both ICFR and audit of financial statements; (4) discuss with management the timeliness of audit and non-audit services provided by the independent auditor; (5) review the audit partner's compensation plans; (6) discuss lead review and partner rotation policies;[30] (7) review auditor independence and related policies and procedures; and (8) discuss the previous inspection reports of the independent auditor.

The SOX requires an audit committee to have authority over and be directly responsible for hiring, compensating, and retaining the company's independent auditor as well as overseeing the work of the independent auditor in issuing audit reports and any related work, and resolving any disagreement between management and the auditor pertaining to financial reporting.[31] To fulfill effectively its EAOF, the audit committee should meet frequently with the company's independent auditor to approve audit and non-audit services provided by the auditor and discuss audit findings and complex accounting matters. The SOX shifted important audit-related responsibilities from management to the audit committee. This shift can reduce potential conflicts of interest between management and the independent auditor, and help in preserving auditor independence. Emerging corporate governance reforms including SOX and listing standards have changed the relationship among audit committee management and external auditors by making the audit committee directly responsible for the appointment of external auditors and holding external auditors ultimately accountable to the audit committee.

The audit committee is charged with overseeing the work of the company's independent auditors and evaluating the performance of independent auditors. In recent years the disclosure of the evaluation of the audit firm has become a norm and best practice.[32] It tripled among S&P 500 and S&P Midcap proxies. This discussion was included within the proposal to ratify the auditor section of the proxy or the audit committee report and was often connected to the appointment of the auditor. S&P 500 companies provided significantly more context around the processes for evaluating the audit firm, tying that discussion to audit firm appointment. The audit committee recognizes the importance of maintaining the independence of the company's independent registered public accounting firm, both in fact and appearance. Each year, the audit committee evaluates the qualifications, performance, and independence of the company's independent registered public accounting firm and determines whether to re-engage the current independent registered public accounting firm. In doing so, the audit committee considers the quality and efficiency of the services provided by the independent registered public accounting firm, its capabilities, and its technical expertise and knowledge of the company's operations and industry.

Audit of Defined Benefit Pensions

Independent auditors are usually engaged to audit the company's employee benefit plans.[33] These types of audit engagements have received considerable attention in the post-SOX era and particularly when significant amounts of pensions and post-retirement benefits are proved to be unfunded. Public companies are required to file an 11-K report with the SEC regarding their employee benefit plans and their independent auditor to issue an audit report on financial statements of benefit plans filed with the SEC.[34] The company's audit committee should pre-approve the audit of defined benefit pension plans and oversee the audit scope and work of the independent auditor in performing such audit services.

Sustainability of the Auditing Profession

The accounting profession worldwide has evolved, adapted over time to many factors and has been shaped by a variety of internal and external influences. One of the most influential factors contributing to the professionalism and refinement of the accounting profession is the certification program. There are a number of certifications in accounting; however, the certified public accountant (CPA) is typically regarded as the mother of all certifications and the highest mark of designation in the global accounting profession. Continuing professional education (CPE) programs are intended to ensure that practicing accountants keep abreast with developments in their profession. The effectiveness of CPE programs depends on their coverage of emerging issues affecting the accounting profession. The accounting profession has recently been faced with increased scrutiny demanding changes in: business sustainability, corporate governance reforms, possible convergence in both accounting and auditing standards, risk assessment, and electronic accounting and auditing process. To meet these challenges, accountants should keep pace with advances and update their technical and soft skills. One way to obtain, secure, and document the required skills is through the CPE programs.

The most practical way to improve audit quality and sustain sustainability of the auditing profession is to hold auditors accountable for their work, particularly when there is a strong evidence of severe audit deficiencies or compromised audit quality. To achieve accountability, the engagement partner should sign the public company financial statement audit under her/his name as it is customary in similar professions (law, medical). Even PCAOB inspection reports in identifying audit deficiencies of public auditors have not identified the auditors of failed audits. Accountability and thus audit quality can be improve if the annual reports of audit firms auditing public companies and registered with the PCAOB be issued on an annual basis. In 2005, the Audit Quality Forum (AQF) identified four indicators (measures) that could improve audit quality and transparency, and foster healthy competition in the accounting profession.[35] These measures are further examined by Rezaee (2009) and include auditor resignation process, auditor engagement letters, shareholder rights to question auditors, and the lead partner's signature on audit reports.[36] These measures are as relevant and unaddressed now as they were a decade ago.

The public disclosure of the audit engagement letters should improve transparency of their content and enable investors to better understand the scope, nature, and terms of the audit that eventually improve auditor accountability and audit quality. Shareholders' rights to question auditors enable investors to communicate with the auditor in a candid manner that may improve audit quality. Public disclosure of information in auditors' resignation letters could provide useful and relevant information for investors to better assess audit quality. As of now, despite the PCAOB continuous efforts, the lead partner signs the audit report in the name of the company's public accounting firm. The requirement of the printed name and signature of the lead partner will bring auditor accountability in line with other professionals and is expected to improve audit quality.[37]

Audit Committee Communication with External Auditors

Successful organizations will recognize the importance of building and sustaining effective relationships among the audit committee and the external auditors. Because they are charged with oversight of external audit function, audit committees are instrumental in determining the amount of support and resources that each group receives. In order to fulfill these responsibilities, frequent and open communication between the audit committee and the auditor is essential. The quality of communication provides opportunities to assess the auditor's performance. The auditor also needs to ensure that this communication takes place to ensure that the audit committee has a complete understanding of the stages of the audit cycle. Such communications should focus on the key accounting or auditing issues that give rise to a greater risk of material misstatement of the financial statements, in addition to any questions or concerns of the audit committee. Regulators may identify a number of matters the auditor must discuss with the audit committee, and it is up to the audit committee to be familiar with those requirements and consider not only whether the auditor made all of the required communications, but, more importantly, the level of openness and quality of these communications.

Auditor Report

The audit report is expected to lend more credibility to financial statements by reducing the information risk that the published financial statements are inaccurate, incomplete, and fraudulent. Investor confidence in financial information promotes the efficiency and attractiveness of capital markets, while misleading information erodes such confidence. Auditors play an important role in our society by adding value to the financial reporting process and by enabling investors to make sound investment decisions, which will make the capital markets more efficient making economic growth and prosperity possible for the nation. However, the current audit report approach "on or off" "comply/do not comply," "Black and White," "pass or fail" audit opinion does not have much value-relevance to investors. Investors demand auditors to express their opinion on overall financial health and future prospects of the company. Auditors then should express their judgment on both financial and non-financial information in a more customized audit report that also reflects the degree of a company's compliance with GAAP.

The current audit reporting model has been criticized for not reflecting auditors' assurance on the quality of financial statements by focusing on a pass/fail approach to audit reporting. The pass/fail approach states whether financial statements are presented fairly in conformity with GAAP (pass) or not (fail). The advantages of this approach are: (1) the audit report has standardized pass/fail language that provides uniformity and improves comparability; and (2) is commonly accepted by the investing public. The disadvantages are: (1) the pass/fail approach does not reflect the quality of the financial statements; (2) this approach does not provide useful information to investors regarding the quality of the company as investment or credit risks; and (3) this approach focuses on fair presentation rather than true and accurate presentation of financial position and results of operations. The current audit report approach of an on or off, comply or do not comply, black or white, pass or fail audit opinion is not value-relevant to investors. Users of financial statements may demand that auditors express their opinion on the overall financial health and future prospects of the company. Auditors should express their judgment on both financial and non-financial information in a more customized audit report.

On June 21, 2011, the PCAOB issued a concept release that is intended to overhaul the auditor's reporting model by suggesting a number of ways to provide more relevant audit information to investors of publicly traded companies. The concept release suggests several changes to the auditor's reporting model and is seeking specific comment on a range of alternatives that could improve audit quality by providing investors with more information about the audit process and more relevant financial and nonfinancial information about public companies. The suggested alternatives are as follows:[38]

1. An auditor's discussion and analysis (AD&A) similar to MD&A. The AD&A will contain information on significant events and matters affecting audit quality such as audit risk, procedures, and results;
2. Required and expanded use of emphasis paragraphs in the audit report discussing most significant matters in the financial statements. These important matters can include discussion about material management judgments, estimates, and measurements;
3. Auditor assurance on other information outside the financial statements. This suggests auditors provide assurance on information outside the financial statements, such as (MD&A), non-GAAP information, or earnings releases; and
4. Clarification of language in the standard auditor's report to reduce the perceived expectation gap of what an audit represents. The perceived areas of expectation gap are in the meaning of reasonable

assurance, auditor responsibility in discovering and reporting fraud, and the auditor responsibility for financial and nonfinancial information outside of the financial statements.

These and other alternative changes in the auditor's reporting model are expected to improve audit quality and reduce the likelihood of audit failures. Audit quality refers to auditor's ability to discover errors, irregularities, and fraud in the financial statements and the willingness to report them. The enhanced audit report will provide useful, relevant, reliable, and transparent financial information to investors and other stakeholders. To make the audit process more transparent and the audit report more relevant, the PCAOB has proposed changes to the auditor's reporting model, including the following: (1) the addition in the auditor's report of a new section in which critical audit matters (CAMs) specific to an audit would be communicated; (2) enhanced language in the auditor's report about the auditor's responsibilities, and new statements in the report intended to communicate more information about the audit and the auditor; and (3) an expansion of the auditor's responsibilities for other information in the annual report, and disclosure about this responsibility in the auditor's report, along with a statement about the results of the new required evaluation of that other information.

The European Union (EU) has approved several audit legislations packages in 2014 that will affect statutory audits for many EU companies.[39] The provisions that have most relevance to audit committees and thus have received considerable attention are mandatory audit firm rotation for EU public interest entities (PIEs) and new prohibitions on non-audit services. In addition, other provisions intended to strengthen the effectiveness and transparency of the audit committees of EU companies, enhance dialogue between auditors and regulators have more direct effect on the formation of audit committees worldwide. These legislations will be effective as of summer 2016. The U.K. Corporate Governance Code was amended in 2013 to include additional requirements including the audit committee report and the external auditor's report. Audit committee reports must discuss material issues relevant to the financial statements and how those issues were addressed. Furthermore, the external auditor's report must discuss the risks that had significant effect on the audit, and how they were addressed in the audit.[40]

Audit Firm Rotation

In the aftermath of the 2007–2009 global financial crisis, policymakers, regulators, and standard-setters worldwide have considered ways to improve audit quality to lend more credibility to published financial statements that influence investor confidence in public financial information and thus the financial market. One suggestion for improving audit quality is to strengthen auditor independence through mandatory audit firm rotation (MAFR). An increasing number of earnings restatements, along with many allegations of financial statement fraud committed by high profile companies, recent financial scandals and crises, have eroded public confidence in corporate governance, the financial reporting process, and audit functions. One of the key provisions of the SOX of 2002, which seeks to restore public confidence, is mandatory periodical audit partner rotation. The prevailing issue has been whether the mandatory audit firm rotation will be effective in resolving the perceived management/auditor conflicts and thus improve audit quality. This issue is motivated by two considerations. First, because any MAFR is costly, it is important to know whether the investing public, for which they are intended, view MAFR as beneficial. Second, global policymakers, regulators, and standard-setters are interested to know whether MAFR is beneficial from the point of view of investor perceptions.

Restoring the public confidence requires a coordinated effort of all members of the global accounting profession including audit firms, accountants, and academicians. The idea of audit firm rotation has been brought up for the purpose of improving auditing quality. MAFR should be considered as an integral part of corporate governance to improve quality, reliability, and transparency of financial reports and credibility, quality, and effectiveness of the related audit functions. Proponent of this concept claims that mandatory auditor rotation would bring more auditor independence and thus would help improve the auditing quality.[41] Opponents of this concept say the cost of the practice is too high, and mandatory rotation of auditors would hurt the auditor in accumulating expertise on certain industries.[42]

The concept of audit firm rotation has been around for some years. In August 2011, the PCAOB issued its Concept Release, which called for mandatory auditor rotation every seven years and later decided to table the idea of mandatory audit firm rotation for auditors of public companies in the United States.[43] Generally, the supporters of audit firm rotation are interested in preserving the independence of the audit firms. The opponents of this idea are citing that the lack of evidence linking audit firm tenure to possible weaknesses in auditor independence and increased cost of audit. The issue of audit firm rotation is extensively and yet inconclusively debated in the literature. The general perception is that audit firm rotation can be very costly, complex, and ineffective without adding much to the objectivity and independence of auditors and audit firms. However, in the post-SOX period many public companies have changed their audit firm, which is roughly a third of all public companies. These suggest that in reality public companies often and frequently change their auditors, and any mandatory audit firm rotation every several years (e.g., 10 years) may not be a bad idea.

Section 203 of SOX and SEC-related rules require the lead and concurring partners to rotate off the company's audit after five years and stay off for five years (five years on, five years off). Audit partners other than the lead and concurring partners involved in an engagement must rotate off after no more than seven years and are subject to a two-year timeout. In selecting the company's public accounting firm, the committee should pay particular attention to auditor independence (e.g., not engaging in prohibited non-audit services), industry specialization, reputation, reasonableness of the audit fee, and requirement for rotation of the lead partner. If the committee at any time becomes aware of a violation of auditor independence, inappropriateness of audit services, significant damages to auditor reputation, or substantial difficulties between management and the independent auditor, the committee should consider changing the company's independent audit firm. However, mandatory rotation of the statutory audit firm will require rotation of the statutory audit firm in Europe after a maximum of 10 years, which can extend this term to 20 years in the case of a competitive tender after the first 10 years or 24 years, in the case of a joint audit regime.[44] New prohibitions on non-audit services provide a detailed list of non-audit services that audit firms and members of their networks may not provide to audit clients including tax services. However, individual EU member states may choose to allow certain tax services given that they have no direct or material effect on the audited financial statements.

Conclusion

The sustainability and financial quality of public companies are important to the safety, liquidity, and efficiency of our capital markets. This chapter addressed the relevance and importance of IFICR as well the roles and responsibilities of the board of directors including the audit committee, management, internal auditors, and external auditors in producing reliable, transparent, and high-quality financial information. In past decade, the PCAOB has actively promoted the role of the audit committee by solicited input from audit committee members on deployment of its standards and has provided resources to support audit committees in effectively executing their duties as stated in the SOX to be "directly responsible for the appointment, compensation, and oversight" of the independent auditor. PCAOB Ethics and Independence Rule 3526 mandates that the audit firm provide relevant information pertaining to its independence to the audit committee before the committee decide to retain the audit firm as its auditors. Audit firms of public companies listed on the New York Stock Exchange are required to annually provide information about their quality control system, internal and external review and investigation of their quality control system, and all relationships with their clients with the audit committee.

The audit committee in the post-Sox era is monitoring auditor independence and competencies in several ways by:

1. Reviewing auditor quarterly review and annual audit of financial statements.
2. Reviewing engagement letters and fees.
3. Approving audit and permissible non-audit services.
4. Reviewing audit plans and overseeing the work performed by auditors.
5. Discussing auditors' judgments on accounting policies and practices.
6. Discussing disagreements with management on accounting policies and practices.

7. Reviewing management letters and recommendations to management.
8. Reviewing internal control assessment by management and auditors.
9. Reviewing significant accounting and auditing risk.
10. Reviewing management antifraud prevention and detection policies and procedures.
11. Reviewing audit procedures in discovering and reporting financial statement fraud.
12. Reviewing auditor's independence policies and practices as pertaining to the working relation with management.

The audit committee oversight function provides an environment where the client auditor relationship is monitored and thus creates an independent environment.

The chair of the audit committee should annually evaluate competency and independence of the company's audit firm with respect to the following:

1. Understanding of the company's business and industry.
2. Preservation of audit firm independence in both fact and appearance.
3. Effective and candid communication with management and the audit committee.
4. Addressing emerging issues, initiatives, developments affecting the company's business, and financial reporting.
5. Resolution of technical business and financial issues in an effective and timely manner.
6. High-quality audit performance throughout the year.

Action Items

1. Ensure compliance with regulatory reforms, and best practices address audit committee oversight function of overseeing the independent auditor.
2. Standard setters including the PCAOB have increasingly reached out to audit committees to solicit their views on various proposals and auditing standards.
3. Oversee independent auditor plan and scope of the audit.

4. Be in charge of hiring, firing, and compensating independent auditors for their approved audit and non-audit services.
5. Provide pre-approval of all audit services and permissible non-audit services.
6. Conduct periodic evaluation and reappointment of independent auditors.

Endnotes

1. The Sarbanes-Oxley Act of 2002. The Public Company Accounting Reform and Investor Protection Act. Available at: www.whitehouse.gov/infocus/corporateresponsibility.
2. Knechel, R., Krishnan, G., Pevzner, M., Shefchik, L., & Velury, U. 2013. Audit Quality: Insights from the Academic Literature. *Auditing: A Journal of Practice & Theory* 32 (Supplement 1): 385–421.
3. Rezaee, Z., & Kedia, B. 2012. The Role of Corporate Governance Participants in Preventing and Detecting Financial statement Fraud. *Journal of Forensic and Investigative Accounting* 4(2).
4. Rezaee, Z. 2004. Corporate governance role in financial reporting. *Research in Accounting Regulation* 2004. 17: 107–114.
5. Center for Audit Quality (CAQ). 2015. External Auditor Assessment Tool. A Reference for Audit Committee Worldwide. Available at: http://thecaq.org/reports-and-publications/external-auditor-assessment-tool-a-reference-for-audit-committees-worldwide
6. DeAngelo, L. E. 1981. Auditor size and audit quality. *Journal of Accounting and Economics* 3(3): 183–199.
7. PCAOB. 2011. *Concept Release on Auditor Independence and Audit Firm Rotation: Notice of Roundtable. PCAOB Release No. 2011-006.* (August 11).Washington, DC: U. S. Public Company Accounting Oversight Board.
8. Public Company Accounting Oversight Board (PCAOB). 2013. *Standing Advisory Group Meeting discussion—audit quality indicators.* Washington, DC: PCAOB.
9. Ibid
10. *PCAOB* Concept Release on Audit Quality Indicators, NO. 2015-005, July 1, 2015.

11. International Auditing and Assurance Standards Board (IAASB). 2014. A Framework for Audit Quality: Key Elements that Creat an Environment for Audit Quality. February 2014. Available at: www .iaasb.org

12. Ibid.

13. PCAOB. 2011. *Concept Release on Auditor Independence and Audit Firm Rotation: Notice of Roundtable. PCAOB Release No. 2011-006.* Washington, DC: U. S. Public Company Accounting Oversight Board, August 11.

14. Center for Audit Quality (CAQ). 2015. Audit Committee Transparency Barometer. Available at: www.the caq.org

15. Ibid.

16. Public Company Accounting Oversight Board (PCAOB). 2003. Auditing Standard No. 1: Reports to the Standards of the Public Company Accounting Oversight Board. Available at: http://pcaobus.org/ Rules_of_the_Board/Documents/Rules_of_the_Board/Auditing_ Standard_1.pdf

17. SOX. Section 201.

18. Ibid.

19. Public Company Accounting Oversight Board. 2004. Auditor Independence and Tax Services (December, proposal). Available at: www.pcaobus.org/Standards/Briefing_Paper%20-%20Independence_Roundtable.pdf

20. Securities and Exchange Commission (SEC). 2003. Disclosure Required by Section 406 and 407 of the Sarbanes-Oxley Act of 2002 (January 23). Rule No. 33-8177. Available at: www.sec.gov/rules/final/shtml

21. Deloitte & Touche. 2003. Audit committee Financial Expert Designation and Disclosure Practice Survey. Available at: www .deloitte.com/dtt/article/0,1002,sid%253D2006%2526cid%2 53D13514,00.html

22. American Institute of Certified Public Accountants (AICPA). 1988. Statement on Auditing Standards (SAS) No 61: Communication with Audit Committees (April). New York.. Public Company Accounting Oversight Board (PCAOB). 2003. Auditing Standard No. 2: An Audit of Internal Control over Financial Reporting Performed in Conjunction with an Audit of Financial Statements.

Available at: http://pcaobus.org/Rules_of_the_Board/Documents/ Rules_of_the_Board/Auditing_Standard_2.pdf.

23. Rezaee, Z. 2007. *Corporate Governance Post-Sarbanes-Oxley*. Hoboken, NJ: John Wiley & Sons.

24. Sarbanes-Oxley Act, 2002.

25. PCAOB Auditing Standard No. 2. 2004 and Auditing Standard No. 5.

26. PCAOB Auditing Standard No 5. An Audit of Internal Control over Financial Reporting that Is Integrated with an Audit of Financial Statements.

27. Ibid.

28. Ibid.

29. Ibid.

30. Under Section 203 of the SOX, the lead audit partner of a public accounting firm auditing a public company must rotate off the engagement after five years. For details see APP *Sarbanes-Oxley Act: Auditor Independence*.

31. SOX Section 301.

32. Ibid.

33. PricewaterhouseCoopers (PwC). 2005. Comparison of Defined Benefit Pension Reform Proposals. PwC's HRS Insight (October 6). Available at: www.cfodirect.com/CFOPrivate.nsf

34. Securities and Exchange Commission (SEC). 2002. Annual Report Pursuant to Section 13 or 15(2) of the Securities Exchange Act of 1934 (September 25). Available at: www.sec.gov/divisions/corpfin/ forms/11-K.htm

35. Audit Quality Forum (AQF). 2005. Audit Quality: Shareholder Involvement Audit Resignation Statements. Institute of Chartered Accountants in England and Wales. Audit and Assurance Faculty (March). Available at: www.icaew.com/index .cfm?route=125705.

36. Rezaee, Z. 2009. *Corporate Governance and Ethics*. Hoboken, NJ: John Wiley & Sons.

37. Ibid.

38. Public Company Accounting Oversight Board (PCAOB). 2011. Concept Release on Possible Revisions to PCAOB Auditing Standards Related to Reports on Audited of Financial Statements.

PCAOB Release No.211-003, June 21, 2011. Available at: www .pcaobus.org

39. Deloitte. Overview of European Union Audit Legislation. Available at: www2.deloitte.com/content/dam/Deloitte/us/Documents/center-for-corporate-governance/us-ccg-eu-audit-legislation-overview-033115.pdf

40. Ibid.

41. American Institute of Certified Public Accountants (AICPA). 2011. Re: Request for Public Comment: Concept Release on Auditor Independence and Audit Firm Rotation. New York.

42. Ibid.

43. Public Company Accounting Oversight Board (PCAOB). 2011. *Concept Release on Auditor Independence and Audit Firm Rotation. Release No. 2011–006.*Washington, DC: PCAOB.

44. See Deloitte.

CHAPTER 4

Internal Audit Oversight Function of the Audit Committee

Executive Summary

The role of internal auditors as an integral part of corporate governance has been evolved from assisting management to providing consulting and assurance services to their organization's corporate governance, risk assessment, and internal controls. The audit committee must oversee the internal audit function including reviewing with the external auditor the responsibilities, staffing, and budget of the internal audit function, and holding executive sessions with the internal auditor. The audit committee can help internal audit add value to the organization by making sure internal audit has the necessary skills and by reinforcing internal audit's stature within the organization and its accountability to the audit committee. This chapter examines the important roles that the audit committee can play in overseeing internal audits' role in corporate governance, financial reporting, and risk assessment, and ensuring they have sufficient skills and resources to effectively do their job.

Introduction

The role of internal auditors as an integral part of corporate governance has been addressed in statements and standards of the Institute of Internal Auditors (IIA).[1] The function of internal audit has evolved from assisting management in discharging its responsibilities to providing assurance and consulting in the areas of financial reporting, auditing, risk assessment, internal control, and corporate governance, and now expressing an opinion on an organization's risk management, governance, and internal controls.[2] In this new capacity, internal auditors conduct an audit and express an opinion on their organization's governance, risk management, and internal controls for the use by the board of directors, management, or external users, other assurance providers, and regulatory bodies.

Internal auditors play an important role in their company's corporate governance, internal control structure, risk management analysis, and financial reporting process. Internal auditors in the post–Sarbanes–Oxley Act (SOX) period have actively been involved in providing management with consulting and assurance services for proper compliance with provisions of SOX, particularly as related to internal controls, risk assessment, and financial reporting. Internal audit resources have also been expanded to satisfy the demand for internal audit services to assist in executive certifications of internal controls and financial reports. Public companies have recognized the important role internal audits play in effective compliance with Section 404 of SOX and have made several adjustments in response to overwhelming demands for internal audit services.[3] However, internal auditors' services to their organizations go beyond assisting in eras of internal controls, financial reporting, and compliance as they have traditionally provided audit services in operational, risk assessment, and nonfinancial activities and quality assurance and improvement programs.

Internal Audit Oversight Function

Internal auditors, in the post-SOX era, have expanded their role beyond internal control assessment and ensuring compliance with applicable laws and regulations to assuming more responsibilities in improving risk management, reducing organizational complexity and costs, and involving strategic and governance processes. Recent years' events have increased the significance of internal audit functions and the role of audit committees in overseeing them. Listing standards of the national stock exchanges (NYSE, NASDAQ) require that listed companies have an internal audit function.[4] Internal auditors increasingly are called upon to assist management in complying with various requirements of SOX. The internal audit function also can assist the audit committee in effectively fulfilling its increased oversight responsibilities over functions besides internal audit. Constructive interactions between the audit committee and the internal auditor can help provide assurance regarding compliance with the provisions of SOX, listing standards, and other emerging corporate governance reforms, and also improve the company's corporate governance.

The increasing interest in and demand for more responsible and effective corporate governance have provided a unique and timely opportunity for internal auditors to improve their audit function. Internal auditors can provide a variety of services to the company's audit committee in understanding management risk assessment, internal control risk, and inherent risk associated with financial statements. The audit committee can also ask internal auditors to assist in the implementation of the audit committee's sponsored whistle-blower programs, code of business conduct, and other activities and programs initiated by the audit committee, or to perform special investigations for the audit committee. Listing standards of national stock exchanges (NYSE, NASDAQ, AMEX) now require (1) their listed companies to have an internal audit function; (2) the audit committee periodically to meet in private without the presence of management with the internal auditor, particularly the CAE; and (3) the internal auditor to inform the audit committee of any areas of concern or need for improvement including financial and audit matters requiring the audit committee attention.[5]

The audit committee should oversee the company's internal audit function by reviewing its resources, independence, authorities, responsibilities, diligence, activities, and performance. To achieve effectiveness in the internal audit and oversight functions, the audit committee should:

1. Hire, compensate, evaluate, and, if necessary, release the company's chief audit executive (CAE; the director of the internal audit department), and oversee the appointment, performance, and termination of other key internal audit personnel. Indeed, the KPMG 2003 survey report indicates that the majority of roundtable participants (over 60 percent) state that their CAE is ultimately appointed and terminated by their audit committee, audit committee chair, or the board of directors.[6]

2. Review and approve the company's internal audit charter including its role, responsibilities, resources, independence, and competence to ensure the charter is in compliance with the guidance and standards of the IIA.[7]

3. Review and approve the budget and staffing for the company's internal audit department.

4. Oversee the cooperation and coordination of audit work between the internal auditor and the independent auditor, particularly in the area of internal control and risk assessment as suggested in the Public Company Accounting Oversight Board (PCAOB) Auditing Standard (AS) No. 2 and its successor AS No. 5.[8]

5. Review the annual evaluation of the company's internal audit function including its reports, assessment, promotion, and rewards.

Internal auditing has transitioned from providing services to management or being viewed as the "eyes and ears" of management to adding value to the organization as an important component of corporate governance. Since SOX and amendments to listing standards, internal audit acts as the "eyes and ears" of the audit committee. An ever-increasing focus on audit committee oversight roles has provided unprecedented opportunities for internal auditors to gain long-awaited recognition as capable of adding value in the corporate governance structure. Internal auditors' close working relationship with the audit committee enables them to: (1) gain better recognition and greater cooperation from management; (2) safeguard their independence; and (3) receive adequate authority and resources to fulfill their assigned responsibilities. This relationship helps the audit committee assess: (1) the company's enterprise risk management pertaining to internal controls, financial reporting, and operations; (2) cooperation and coordination of audit activities between internal auditors and external auditors; and (3) unusual and risky transactions and events.

The audit committee is responsible for overseeing the effectiveness of the internal audit function in achieving its goal of adding value to the organization. This internal audit oversight function consists of overseeing the company's internal audit function including its charter, budget, staffing, audit plans, audit activities, and reports.

1. Overseeing Internal Audit Charter: The purpose, authority, role, and responsibility of the company's internal audit function are usually described in its charter. The internal audit charter specifies the mission, scope of work, independence, authority, responsibilities, standards, and accountability of the company's internal audit function. The audit committee is responsible for reviewing the internal audit charter to ensure whether it is suitable for the company, is tailored to the internal audit needs of the company, and specifies internal audit purpose, authority, responsibility, activities, and accountability. The written internal audit charter should be reviewed and approved by the audit committee and signed by the chairperson of the audit committee. Exhibit 4.1 presents responsibilities of the audit committee regarding the internal audit function as stated in the audit committee charters of several public companies including FedEx, Target, Mattel, Eastman, Kodak, and 3M.

2. Overseeing Budget and Staffing of Internal Audit Function: The effectiveness of the internal audit function depends on the adequacy of its financial resources and human capital. The internal audit function should have sufficient financial resources to employ adequate, competent, and ethical staff to effectively carry out its assigned responsibilities. The competency, integrity, objectivity, and independence of the director of the internal audit function—commonly referred to as "the chief audit executive, CAE"—can play an important role in ensuring the effectiveness of the company's internal audit function. Thus, the audit committee should review and approve the appointment, compensation, and termination of the CAE. The audit committee should oversee the annual evaluation of the internal audit function, particularly the assessment of the performance of the CAE. The audit committee should also assess whether the internal audit function is adequate and effective in providing the company's internal audit services related to internal controls, operational efficiency, financial reporting, and compliance with applicable laws and regulations.

3. Overseeing Internal Audit Plans and Activities: The audit committee should periodically review and approve internal audit plans and activities to ensure that the internal audit function adds value to

the company. The audit committee should ensure that internal audit plans and the scope of activities respond to the company's overall enterprise risk management, focus on both operational and financial audits, provide sufficient coverage of all company's reporting units (departments, divisions, functional units), and are properly coordinated with the audit of internal control over financial reporting (ICFR) and financial statements conducted by the independent auditor. Internal auditors should be flexible enough to respond properly to emerging and unanticipated events and provide other relevant services to the audit committee. Example of services internal auditors can provide to the audit committee are design and implementation of whistle-blower programs, code of conduct, performance of specified investigations for the audit committee, providing in-house training for audit committee members, and preparing audit committee meetings.

4. Overseeing Accountability of Internal Audit Function: Internal auditors should be held accountable for their decisions, actions, and activities, and the audit committee should oversee their work. To ensure accountability of the internal audit function, the audit committee should: (1) monitor the independence and objectivity of the internal audit function, particularly that of the CAE: (2) periodically evaluate the performance of internal audit function; (3) receive and review internal audit activity reports relevant to audit findings, strengths, weakness, recommendations, and management responses to those findings; (4) ensure the internal audit function fulfills its assigned responsibilities and is in compliance with its professional standards and codes of ethical conduct; and (5) perform effectively within the provided budget.[9]

A close working relationship between the audit committee and internal auditors can improve the effectiveness of corporate governance.[10] First, the independence and objectivity of internal auditors can be strengthened when they report their findings and opinions directly to the audit committee. Second, the prestige and status of internal auditors can be enhanced when they work with management at all levels while being accountable to the audit committees. Third, internal auditors can be of a

Exhibit 4.1

Responsibilities of the audit committee regarding the internal audit function as stated in the audit committee charter

FedEx Corporation[1]	Target Corporation[2]	3M Company[3]
a. Review the appointment and replacement, and annually review the performance of the senior internal auditing executive.	a. Review and discuss with the head of internal audit the approach to risk assessment in the development of the annual audit plan, including the risk of fraud, and the commitment of internal audit resources to audit the Corporation's guidelines-policies, and procedures to mitigate identified risks.	a. Periodically review the charter, annual plan, and scope of work of internal audit, including its responsibilities and staffing.
b. Periodically review and discuss with the independent auditor the organizational structure, responsibilities, budget, and staffing of the internal audit department.		b. Periodically review the results of internal audits and management's response thereto, and discuss related significant ICFR matters with the company's internal auditor and company management.
c. Review the annual audit plan of the internal audit department and the results of any audits that are significant to the company's system of internal controls and management's responses to such reports.	b. Discuss the internal audit department's responsibilities, annual audit plan, budget, and staffing with the head of internal audit.	c. Discuss the adequacy of the company's internal controls with internal audit.
	c. Review significant internal audit results and management's action plans.	d. Review the appointment, replacement and reassignment, and periodically evaluate the performance of the senior internal auditing executive, who shall have direct reporting obligations to the Committee.
	d. Periodically review the charter for the internal audit function.	

[1] Available at: http://investors.fedex.com/English/governance-and-citizenship/committee-charters/audit-committee-charter/default.aspx
[2] Available at: http://media.corporate-ir.net/media_files/irol/65/65828/corpgov/auditPD.pdf
[3] Available at: http://s2.q4cdn.com/974527301/files/doc_downloads/gov_docs/Audit-Committee-Charter-Bd02032015.pdf

significant assistance to audit committees to effectively fulfill their oversight duties in functions such as financial reporting, internal controls, risk management, external audit, whistle-blowing, ethics, and taxes.

Internal Auditors and Internal Controls

Internal auditors have traditionally used a risk-based approach in performing audits of controls over their company's operational effectiveness, reliability of financial reports, and compliance with applicable laws, rules, and regulations. Section 404 of SOX and PCAOBAS Nos. 2 and 5 encourage internal auditors to focus on compliance-driven controls in assisting management in the preparation of reports on ICFR. Section 302 of SOX requires quarterly management certifications of both financial statements and financial reporting controls, whereas Section 404 requires annual management assessment of the effectiveness of both the design and operation of ICFR. While management's responsibilities for compliance with both Sections 302 and 404 cannot be delegated or abdicated, internal auditors can considerably assist management in fulfilling their compliance responsibilities. Many companies, in an attempt to comply with the requirements of Section 404 and AS No. 2 on management reporting on internal controls, turned to their internal auditors for documentation of the effectiveness of both design and operation of their ICFR. Management is primarily responsible for the design, implementation, and maintenance of ICFR, and internal auditors provide assurance and opine on internal control. Internal auditors in assisting management should maintain their objectivity and independence according to their charter and properly communicate with the audit committee. The CAE should consult with the audit committee in devoting internal audit resources to Sections 302 and 404 without compartmentalizing their other internal audit activities, while adding value to their organization's performance.

Section 404 of SOX makes management of a public company responsible for establishing and maintaining an adequate internal control structure and procedures for financial reporting. Section 404 also directs the Securities and Exchange Commission (SEC) to prescribe rules requiring each annual report of a public company to contain an internal control report. Under SEC rules implementing Section 404, management's report on ICFR must include the following:

1. A statement of management's responsibility for establishing and monitoring adequate and effective ICFR.

2. A statement of management's assessment of the effectiveness of design and operation of ICFR as of the end of the company's most recent fiscal year.
3. A statement identifying the framework (e.g., COSO) used by management to assess the effectiveness of ICFR.
4. A statement that the company's independent auditor has attested to and reported on management's assessment of ICFR.
5. Management disclosure of any material weakness in ICFR.[11]

The audit committee should oversee the company's compliance with section 404. The audit committee should work with management, internal auditors, the independent auditor, and even outside service providers to design internal control programs tailored to the company's internal control structure and the financial reporting process by: (1) identifying the company's key transaction cycles; (2) documenting process flows for key transaction cycles; (3) establishing internal controls for key transaction cycles; (4) performing walkthrough procedures for key transaction cycles; (5) performing tests of controls on key transaction cycles; (6) identifying potential significant deficiencies and material weaknesses; (7) redesigning internal controls for key transaction cycles by correcting significant deficiencies and material weaknesses; (8) retesting and improving internal controls; (9) assessing the effectiveness of ICFR; (10) assisting in the preparation of executive certification of ICFR in compliance with Section 404 of SOX and SEC rules.

Deloitte and Touche (2004) suggests that audit committees consider asking the following questions to understand and evaluate the strength of their company's internal control management program[12]:

1. Is the company's Section 404 compliance project directed from and supported by the executives?
2. Does the company have continuous enterprise standards for internal control assessment and management?
3. Is there a formal training program to educate affected employees regarding their Section 404 responsibility and effective fulfillment of such responsibilities?
4. Does the company's technology infrastructure adequately support Section 404 compliance and identified risks?

5. Has the company assigned responsibilities for the assessment of overall financial reporting risk to the appropriate group?

6. Are key financial reporting risks consistently identified, prioritized, controlled, and communicated throughout the company?

7. Do employees have sufficient understanding of the financial reporting risks associated with their business areas, activities, and performance, and do they implement relevant control activities?

8. In overseeing the company's compliance with Section 404, should the audit committee satisfy itself that these and other pertinent questions have been answered?

Section 404 of SOX, the SEC's implementing rule, and PCAOB AS Nos. 2 and 5 have enhanced the audit committee oversight function over internal controls in many ways, including: (1) overseeing management annual reports on ICFR; (2) management communication of internal control issues, concerns, and limitations to independent auditors; and (3) management corrections of material internal control weaknesses identified in the auditor's report on ICFR. PCAOB AS No. 2 requires the independent auditor to communicate to management and the audit committee all significant deficiencies and material weaknesses identified during the audit of ICFR.[13] Such communication should: (1) distinguish between those controls that are considered significant deficiencies and those that are classified as material weaknesses; (2) be in writing; and (3) be made prior to the issuance of audit reports on ICFR or an integrated audit report on both the financial statements and internal controls.

The extent of internal auditors' involvement with Sections 302 and 404 depends on the company's internal auditing function, resources, funding, personnel qualifications, and charter. Any activities performed by internal auditors should be in compliance with their charter, professional standards, and mission of adding value to their organization's operations. The IIA's 2004 position paper suggests the following factors be considered: (1) consulting management on internal control activities does not impair the internal auditor's independence and objectivity; (2) making key management decisions in the internal control compliance process impairs the internal auditor's objectivity and independence; (3) having responsibility for specific operations or participation in directing key management decisions impairs the internal auditor's objectivity and independence; (4) the design, implementation, and drafting procedures for internal controls to comply with Sections 302 and 404 impair the internal auditor's independence and objectivity; (5) recommendations of standards for internal controls or reviews of internal control procedures do not impair the internal auditor's objectivity and independence; and (6) devoting a significant amount of effort to consult with management on Sections 302 and 404 compliance can deplete internal auditors' resources and deviate their attention from other value-adding activities.[14]

A 2007 PwC survey reveals that: (1) more than 36 percent of the CAEs reported issuing an annual overall opinion on internal controls; and (2) about 26 percent of the CAEs provided an annual overall opinion on internal controls.[15] In expressing an opinion on internal controls, internal auditors should assess the current status of internal audit opinion (IAO), possible challenges and opportunities in IAO, recommendations and remediation actions to improve internal controls, management's willingness and commitment to implement remedial actions, and internal auditors' understanding of objectives and limitations of IAO. The quality and reliability of IAO depend on transparency, constructive recommendations, and the objectivity, independence, and organizational status of the CAE signing the report. To be relevant, internal auditor opinions and recommendations should be related to identify risks and intended controls to address risks, and be constructive, reliable, clear, concise, and relevant in making recommendations and remediating actions in improving the effectiveness of the design and operation of internal controls.

Internal auditors, particularly the CAEs, should exercise caution in expressing an opinion on their organizations' overall internal controls or specifically on ICFR, ensure that their objectivity and independence are not compromised, and not assume responsibility for management certification of ICFR. In expressing an opinion on ICFR, internal auditors should carefully consider and follow the guidance issued by the IIA, *Practical Considerations Regarding Internal Auditing Expressing an Opinion on Internal Control.*[16]

Conclusion

Internal auditors are well positioned to work and make recommendations to management regarding the design, implementation, and maintenance of effective internal controls and expressing an opinion on internal control by: (1) developing and maintaining an internal control system that is adequate and effective in managing risks; (2) improving the efficiency and effectiveness of risk management processes and controls; (3) reviewing entity-level controls relevant to the company's integrity and ethical values, management's philosophy and operating style, organizational structure, human resources policies and procedures, competence and integrity of personnel, and assignment of authority and responsibility; (4) challenging management's decisions pertaining to internal control where appropriate; and (5) facilitating improvements in the internal control structure by working with the company's board of directors, audit committee, and management.

Internal auditors should conduct themselves in a way that would not threaten their independence or objectivity or put themselves in a position to assess their own work. To maintain their independence and objectivity, internal auditors should be appropriately positioned within the organization, be overseen by the audit committee, have reporting lines and adequate resources approved by the board of directors, and have unrestricted access to people, records, and information throughout the organization. Proper communication between internal auditors, external auditors, and the audit committee is essential in improving the effectiveness and efficiency of the internal audit function.

Action Items

1. Review and approve charter of the internal audit department.
2. Select, hire, fire, and compensate the CAE who is chairing the internal audit department.
3. Have the internal audit department directly and functionally report to the audit committee.
4. Review and approve the internal audit department's audit strategies, planning, scope of the audit, and work.

5. Assess the performance of the internal audit department and the CAE periodically.

6. Review the budget of the internal audit department periodically

Endnotes

1. The Institute of Internal Auditors (IIA). 2002. Recommendations for Improving Corporate Governance: A Position Paper Presented by the IIA to the U.S. Congress (April 8). Available at: www.theiia. org/download.cfm?file=1609

2. The Institute of Internal Auditors (IIA). 2009. New Guidance for Formulating and Expressing Internal Audit Opinions (April 16).

3. Rezaee, Z. 2007. *Corporate governance post –Sarbanes-Oxley: Regulators, Requirements, and Integrated Processes*. Hoboken, NJ: Wiley & Sons Inc.

4. New York Stock Exchange (NYSE). 2004. Final NYSE Corporate Governance Rules. Available at: www.ecgi.org/codes/documents/ finalcorpgovrules.pdf

5. Ibid.

6. KPMG. 2003. Audit Committee Roundtable: Building a Framework for Effective Audit Committee Oversight. KPMG's Audit Committee Institute (Spring). Available at: www.kpmg.com/aci

7. Institute of Internal Auditors (IIA). 2005. Professional Practices Framework. Available at: www.theiia.org/bookstore.cfm

8. Public Company Accounting Oversight Board (PCAOB). 2004. Auditing Standard (AS) No. 2: An Audit of Internal Control over Financial Reporting Performed in Conjunction with an Audit of Financial Statements. (March 9). Available at: http://pcaobus.org/ Standards/Auditing/Pages/Auditing_Standard_2.aspx

9. For details about the internal audit function, see _____ APP, *Internal Auditing: General Principles and Best Practices*.

10. Rezaee, 2007

11. Securities and Exchange Commission (SEC). 2003. Manager's Report on Internal Control over Financial Reporting and Certification of Disclosure in Exchange Act Periodic Reports. Release No 34-47986 (June 5). Available at: www.sec.gov/rules/final/33-8238.htm

12. Deloitte & Touche. 2004. Sarbanes-Oxley Section 404: 10 Threats to Compliance. Available at: www2.deloitte.com/content/dam/Deloitte/us/Documents/audit/us-aers-assur-ten-threats-sep2004.pdf

13. PCAOB Auditing Standard No.2. 2004.

14. The Institute of Internal Auditors (IIA). 2005. Re: Implementation of U.S. Sarbanes-Oxley Act Internal Control Provisions (March 31). Available at: www.theiia.org/download.cfm?file=73806

15. PricewaterhouseCoopers. 2007. State of internal audit profession study: Pressures build for continual focus on risk (May). Available at: www.pwc.com/internalaudit

   The Institute of Internal Auditors (IIA). 2005. Practical Considerations Regarding Internal Auditing Expressing an Opinion on Internal Control (June 10). Available at: www.theiia.org/download .cfm?file=25663Internal Audit Oversight Function of the Audit Committee

CHAPTER 5

Risk Management Oversight Function of the Audit Committee

Executive Summary

Organizations of all types, sizes, and complexities are facing a variety of risks that should be managed through effective risk management systems and internal controls. These risks and their effective assessment and monitoring affect the reliability of financial statements and effectiveness of internal controls. Management, external auditors, and internal auditors can provide assurance to the audit committee on the managerial process designed to manage the risks and minimize their impacts on financial reporting and auditing processes. The audit committee should oversee the company's risk assessment and management to provide assurance on the processes designed to manage risk, implement effective internal controls, and produce reliable financial statements. The audit committee assists the board of directors, management, and external auditors by reviewing and evaluating the effectiveness of the risk management process and internal controls designed to manage the key risks affecting the organization's financial reporting and internaål controls. This chapter discusses the audit committee review of the company's risk assessment and management.

Introduction

Oversight of a company's risk processes is a significant role, and it requires an understanding of the company's processes to identify, assess, manage, mitigate, and communicate risk throughout the company.

Because this is such a significant role, it is typically assigned to the audit committee. The environment in which a company conducts its business can directly affect its corporate governance and the way it is managed. The environment also affects the company's risks, which should be identified and managed. The audit committee should understand the company's environment, the risks associated with its operations, how management is responding to risks, and the potential impacts on the integrity of financial reporting.

The audit committee's primary responsibilities consist of overseeing financial reporting and controls and external and internal auditors. However, the aftermath of the 2007–2009 global financial crisis, which were primarily caused with management's excessive and aggressive risk-taking practices and appetite, has led the audit committees to pay more attention to the company's risk assessment and management. Each company is subject to varying risks driven from uncertainty relevant to its operations, events, transactions, and environment. The economic situation, the industry, market conditions, management capabilities, business and operating activities, financial stability, and corporate governance structure all contribute to a company's appetite and tolerance for risk. All of these factors directly affect the audit committee's responsibilities in overseeing internal control, financial reporting, and audit activities. The audit committee should meet regularly with management to discuss the company's enterprise risk management (ERM), its strategy, operating, financial reporting, and compliance objectives, and procedures for achieving them, related control activities, and assessment of the progress toward their achievements. This remainder of this chapter examines this risk assessment oversight function of the audit committee.

Risk Management Oversight Function

The emerging corporate governance reforms encourage companies to take a proactive approach in preventing and detecting financial failures by engaging in ERM activities. The Committee of Sponsoring Organizations of the Treadway Commission (COSO), in September 2004, issued its Enterprise Risk Management Integrated Framework that presents a model of the ERM and defines ERM as:

A process, affected by an entity's board of directors, management, and other personnel, applied in strategy setting and across the enterprise, designed to identify potential events that may affect the entity, and manage risks to be within its risk appetite, to provide reasonable assurance regarding the achievement of entity objectives.[1]

The above definition implies that ERM is a systematic and ongoing process involving the entity's board and management identifying events that affect the entity, and managing their risk within its stakeholder appetite for risk, to achieve the entity's strategic, operational, reporting, and compliance objectives. ERM is a continuous process of identifying, assessing, and informing corporate directors, the audit committee, and executives of the quantified risks that challenge the company, their potential losses and possible rewards. The ERM focuses on identifying events and managing their risk to achieve the objectives pertaining to strategy, operations, financial reporting, and compliance with applicable laws and regulation. The ERM framework identifies eight key components that facilitate an effective ERM process. Many risk-related issues are associated with reported corporate and accounting scandals (e.g., Enron, WorldCom, Global Crossing, and Qwest). The 2007–2009 global financial crisis can be attributed to many factors including an inadequate risk assessment of business transactions and their risk management. In the wake of these financial scandals and crises, ERM has received tremendous attention as a new measure for managing risk. Thus, risk management has become an integral component of oversight and managerial functions affecting every transaction and economic event. Exhibit 5.1 summarizes objectives and key components of COSO's ERM framework.

ERM at General Motors

General Motors (GM) uses ERM to identify its risks related to legal, market, currency, interest rate, and commodity price and to manage these risks within its risk appetite to achieve its strategic, operational, financial reporting, and compliance objectives. GM, like other automobile makers, is exposed to legal risk associated with materials used in its production, product safety risk, fluctuations in foreign currency exchange rates, changes in interest rates, and certain commodity and equity prices.[2]

Exhibit 5.1

Components of ERM

Component	Description
1. Internal Environment	The foundation of ERM
2. Objective Setting	Strategic goals and mission
3. Event Identification	Internal and external factors affecting objectives
4. Risk Assessment	Likelihood and impact of potential events
5. Risk Response	Risk tolerance
6. Control Activities	Policies and procedures
7. Information and Communication	From internal and external sources
8. Monitoring	Ongoing basis, periodic

Source: Adapted from Committee of Sponsoring Organizations (COSO). 2004. Enterprise Risk Management-Integrated Framework. Available at: www.coso.org

To manage these risks, GM has used ERM and a risk management control system to monitor risks, and a sensitivity analysis in determining the fair value of financial instruments recorded on its consolidated balance sheet. Exhibit 5.2 describes the steps to be taken by management to successfully complete the implementation of ERM.

The Audit Committee Role in ERM

The importance of the systematic risk assessment and management through ERM can also be found in the recent Dodd–Frank Financial Reform (DOF) Act of 2010, which requires organizations to place sufficient focus on compliance risk.[3] In the post-DOF era, public companies in general and financial institutions in particular should integrate risk management into their ERM assessment process and thus underscore the importance of ERM and risk assessment and its integration into the corporate governance function. Specifically, the DOF of 2010 requires large financial institutions (over $10 billion in assets) to have either a formal board-level risk committee that oversees the identification and assessment of the institution's risk management or a risk compliance executive position (Dodd–Frank Act, 2010, Section 165).[4] Public companies should

Exhibit 5.2

Common steps taken by managements to successfully complete the implementation of ERM

1. Core Team Preparedness
   - Organize a core team consisting of members from a variety of business units
   - The team should become experts on the COSO ERM framework's components and principles
   - The expertise thus allows the team to design and implement a unique ERM process for their specific organization or entity
2. Executive Sponsorship
   - It is essential that involvement by key executives is initiated in the implementation process
   - The executive involvement and leadership helps express the benefits that ERM provides and validates the investment of resources
3. Implementation Plan Development
   - A plan is set in place defining the key project phases that include work streams, resources, and timing
   - Responsibilities are identified, followed by the establishment of a project management system.
   - The plan's primary purpose is to allow for the constant communication between team leadership, maintaining the progress of the various units and personnel involved, and analyzing the potential entity-wide changes created by ERM implementation
4. Current State Assessment
   - Asses the application of the ERM components, concepts, and principles and their effectiveness
   - This is also a step where the core team identifies formal and informal policies, processes, practices, and techniques already in place, and also existing capabilities in the organization for applying the COSO ERM framework's principles and concepts

(Continued)

Exhibit 5.2 (*Continued*)

5. Enterprise Risk Management Vision
   - A vision and strategy is developed by the core team that outlines how ERM will be utilized and how it will be incorporated within the organization to accomplish its objectives
   - Identified organization objectives include: (1) how the organization focuses its enterprise risk management efforts on aligning risk appetite and strategy; (2) enhancing risk response decisions; (3) identifying and managing cross-enterprise risks; (4) seizing opportunities; and (5) improving deployment of capital
6. Capability Development
   - Steps 4 & 5 contribute to the assessment of the existing and functioning people, technology, and process capabilities, while also identifying additional capabilities tending to be:
     ○ Defining roles and responsibilities
     ○ Modifications to the organizational model, policies, processes, methodologies, tools, techniques, information flows, and technologies
7. Implementation Plan
   - The original plan is updated and enhanced, adding depth and breadth to cover further assessment, design, and deployment
   - Additional responsibilities are defined
   - Project management system is refined (as necessary)
8. Change Management Development and Deployment
   - Certain actions are developed to implement and sustain the ERM Vision and desired capabilities, including: deployment plans, training sessions, reward reinforcement mechanisms, and monitoring the remainder of the implementation process
9. Monitoring
   - Management will continuously review and improve risk management capabilities

Source: Enterprise Risk Management – Integrated Framework: Application Techniques. September 2004. The Committee of Sponsoring Organizations of the Treadway Commission. pg. 3–4.

evaluate their corporate governance characteristics and financial reporting attributed in determining whether board oversight of risk management or executive risk management position serve them better. The important thing is that it does not really matter who is responsible on the board for overseeing risk management and it could be the audit committee or risk compliance committee. It is better to have the entire board review and approve the company's risk oversight than to delegate this important risk management oversight function to an audit or risk committee. Although the reputation, systemic, strategic, and operational risk can be overseen by the entire board of directors, financial risks are generally overseen by the audit committee, and other risks go to other committees where the expertise is, but overall the entire board of directors has to review and approve the company's risk management. Communication between the board and senior management is extremely important to determine who is in charge of risk assessment and management.

Once the risks—either strategic, operational, reputational, or financial—are identified, a risk expert or a group of experts needs to be hired. The board of directors should have a complete understanding of risk and then assign either a risk board committee or risk compliance executive position to ensure proper risk assessment and management. Risk is a responsibility of the audit committee where risk is traditionally seen as financial risk or credit risk. As the number of risks being faced expands, the notion that it should be the board audit committee oversight responsibility may not be appropriate. Audit committees do not typically have risk management expertise outside of financial risks. Furthermore, listing standards of the New York Stock Exchange in 2003 require the audit committee to explain the strategies and policies which they use in risk assessment and management[5]. Standard and Poor's had started using ERM analysis in its global corporate credit rating process in 2008.[6]

The audit committee should review the company's ERM to learn about: (1) the nature and extent of risks associated with the company's operations and financial reporting; (2) management risk appetite and tolerance and whether the assumed risk appetite is acceptable and prudent; (3) the likelihood of the occurrence of risks; (4) the ability of the company to reduce the incidents and effects of the risks threatening its operations and financial reporting; (5) internal control activities designed to manage the risks; (6) cost–benefit effectiveness of the designed internal control activities; and (7) internal and external auditors' assessment of the effectiveness of both the design and operations of internal control activities to address these risks and periodic reporting of this assessment to the audit committee. The audit committee should oversee all types of risks facing the company involving operational, functional, technology, business, strategic risks, and fraudulent financial reporting risks.

The audit committee has moved from acting as a liaison between management and external auditors to preserve auditor independence to a new oversight function of focusing on adding value to corporate governance, financial reporting, internal controls, and risk management. Under this broadened oversight function, audit committees can assist their organizations by closely working with management and internal auditors to identify, assess, and manage risks. Thus, audit committees (through their oversight function) can make considerable contributions to the ERM process and its implementation. The chief audit executive (CAE) can assume responsibility for the proper design of the ERM concept and obtain a firm commitment from the board of directors, the audit committee, and top executives for effective implementation of ERM in addressing the organization's risk profiles, appetite, exposure, and controls. Effective design and operation of the ERM concept requires commitment and oversight responsibility from the full board of directors and the audit committee, and proactive participation from top executives and internal auditors in implementing ERM.

Effective design and operation of ERM can improve corporate governance in several ways. First, it can improve the oversight function of the board of directors and the audit committee by better informing directors of the organization's risk profiles, exposures, appetite, assessments, and management. Second, it can assist management in achieving accountability by creating a better understanding of major business events, their risks and rewards, and plans to manage the risk. Third, it can strengthen the internal audit function by assuming a consultative approach of educating and training operating personnel to implement ERM.

The audit committee should oversee the design, implementation, and operation of ERM and receive a progress report on ERM from internal auditors. This report should highlight the organization's major risks, managerial plans to manage risks, and its impacts on creating stakeholder value. The board of directors and the audit committee should be informed regarding the organization's overall risk profiles, exposures, appetite, assessment, and controls. To properly address this issue, the audit committee should consider these areas of focus[7]:

- How does the board allocate among its committees the responsibility for oversight of the major substantive areas of risk, as well as responsibility for oversight of the company's risk management processes?
- How have board governance and oversight processes changed, and advanced, as the business and risk environment has become more complex?
- Given the time required to carry out its core responsibilities, what risk oversight responsibilities are appropriate for the audit committee?

Risk oversight responsibilities that are appropriate for the audit committee vary from company to company. In addition to financial statement and disclosure risks, the audit committee may focus on one or more of the following risks: (1) legal/regulatory compliance, including Foreign Corrupt Practice Act risk; (2) tax risk; (3) finance, liquidity, and capital structure risks; and (4) cybersecurity, data privacy, and other information technology (IT)–related risks.[8]

Audit committees should understand not only their company's management risk appetite and tolerance but also management's risk assessment policies and procedures. The audit committee should assess the effectiveness of the company's internal controls to identify, assess, respond, and mitigate risks associated with both the external and internal environment. The audit committee should consider and discuss with management and internal auditors the following external conditions and events that may increase the company's risk: (1) globalization and competition in global markets; (2) economic conditions and stability; (3) ever-increasing technological changes and advances; (4) possible downturns in the industry; (5) market shares for the company's products and services; (6) unrealistic earnings performance and expectations by market participants, including investors and analysts; and (7) high interest rates and currency exposures.

The audit committee should also be aware of risks associated with the company's corporate governance and structure including: (1) ineffective corporate governance structure; (2) a dominant CEO who exerts unusual pressure on senior management to achieve unrealistic goals; (3) frequent organizational changes including high turnover of senior executives and other key personnel; (4) overly complex organizational structures and business transactions; (5) unjustifiable managerial risk appetite and tolerance; (6) unreasonable and inappropriate performance, financial results, or trends in earnings. Helping to ensure that the company is headed in the right direction and is taking appropriate risks is a role that requires deeper engagement as the business and risk environment becomes more complex and faster paced.

In an edition of Global Boardroom Insights, seasoned directors and risk professionals share their thoughts on how boards are strengthening their oversight of risk. Key interview insights the following: (1) Good risk management is an ongoing business discussion—dynamic and enterprise-wide; (2) Risk and strategy go hand in hand; (3) Getting the risk culture right starts at the top but succeeds in the middle; (4) Recognize that cyber security is a critical business risk, requiring the full board's attention; and (5) Step back and assess whether risk oversight roles and responsibilities are clear and still make sense.[9]

Audit committees should consider the inherent risk associated with the company's financial reporting and the control risk of its internal control system, including: (1) the extent of income-increasing or income-decreasing earnings management by senior executives; (2) identified significant deficiencies and material weaknesses in the company's internal controls; (3) senior executives' attitude toward and preferences for making conservative versus liberal choices of accounting alternatives, policies, procedures, and accounting for estimates and reserves; (4) possibility of management override of internal controls; (5) inappropriate and untimely response by management to the identified significant deficiencies and material weaknesses in internal control over financial reporting; (6) any unwarranted delay or lack of compliance with provisions of Sarbanes–Oxley Act (SOX) and Securities and Exchange Commission (SEC) implementing rules, particularly Section 404 compliance; (7) significant unresolved disputes or disagreements between management and the independent auditor over accounting policies, practices, or internal controls; (8) all alternative treatments of financial information within generally accepted accounting principles; and (9) significant written communications between management and the independent auditor.

Internal Auditors and ERM

Internal auditors are focusing more on effective risk assessments and the use of a risk-based approach in their audit coverage by: (1) adopting a process approach to risk assessment and planning; (2) supplementing annual risk assessments with quarterly or more frequent updates; (3) leveraging prior assessment results; (4) aligning risk assessments; (5) obtaining the needed specialized talent; and (6) coordinating with other risk management groups.[10]

Internal auditors in using the IIA guidelines should: (1) assess the entire risk management profile of their organization, including risks related to financial reporting, operations, strategy, and information technology; (2) prioritize risk management categories in terms of their threads to their organizations' sustainable performance; (3) work with senior management and the audit committee in the assessment process to address risks and minimize their effects; (4) establish a risk-based internal audit plan based on an enterprise-wide risk management assessment; and (5) formulate opinions and communicate findings to the audit committee, management, and other applicable stakeholders.

In 2015, Grant Thornton LLP conducted the "Governance, Risk, and Compliance Survey," which surveyed both CAEs and audit committee members.[11] The responses suggest that CAEs and audit committee members see internal audit priorities differently. Asked to rank their focus on four types of risks, audit committee members cited their priorities as follows: financial, compliance, operational, and strategic risks. CAEs ranked the risks as follows: compliance, operational, financial, and strategic risks.

Asked about areas where they wanted internal audit to deliver value, audit committee members ranked "mitigating risk" first, while CAEs ranked "identifying improvement opportunities" first. By prioritizing mitigating risk, audit committees signaled that they understand their oversight responsibilities over the organization's financial reporting. These findings also underscore the idea that CAEs are eager to rebalance or even disproportionately shift activities and concentrate more on bringing a consultative approach to auditing and focusing on adding greater value in areas such as operational auditing. With this data, it is evident that there is a prioritization misalignment.

Internal audit priorities can be rebalanced by optimizing compliance activities. Optimizing compliance is a term that refers to an integrated approach to efficiently and effectively identifying risks and testing controls in a way that allows organizations to achieve greater comfort with less effort. This allows organizations to streamline compliance testing and provide a sustainable framework for long-term compliance management. Other benefits of internal audit and compliance optimization include: true responsiveness to regulatory requirements and remediation demands; integration of risk identification and monitoring predictive analytics; internal audit and forensic disciplines, allowing focus on the delivery of principles and objectives; decreased reporting cycles; improved visibility and optimization for the allocation of compliance resources; consideration of how governance, risk and compliance (GRC) technology can assist in optimizing coverage and efficiencies; and integration of both financial and operational data into a unified regulatory reporting framework.

Successfully optimizing compliance activities requires an integrated approach that allows internal audit to get the most out of compliance activities, and thus enabling a focus on more value-added activities. To enhance the financial controls and compliance effort, CAEs should engage in the following actions: (1) Leverage control testing across multiple compliance areas in a "one to many" approach; (2) Use GRC technology, along with data analytics, for more automated, continual, and predictive control monitoring and reporting activities; (3) Implement the 2013 COSO Internal Control Integrated Framework; and (4) Leverage an enterprise-wide view of risks and controls.

The one-to-many approach is to test once but report on multiple compliance requirements while remediating any regulatory gaps. This will allow organizations to streamline some of their compliance testing, meet more regulatory requirements, provide a sustainable framework for long-term compliance management, and reduce redundancies and focus on delivering objectives, all without repeating the same testing activities in a short period of time, in the same areas, but for different mandates.

Although internal audit departments are eager to improve the efficiency of the internal audit function, many of these departments are not adopting enabling technologies to the degree that might be expected. According to the survey, only 28% of CAEs noted that their organizations are using a GRC/internal audit–specific technology tool. CAEs whose departments are using this technology explained that they're primarily using it for internal audit function management and administration, centralized management and reporting of audit plans and results, enterprise-wide risk management, and SOX testing. Those who don't use this technology explained that the cost and time required to deploy the technology was the primary implementation challenge, followed by the cost of seat licenses and poor fit with requirements. Forty-seven percent of respondents noted that they are using data analytics to enhance the internal audit function. Benefits cited by respondents include: a more efficient internal audit process; support of optimization efforts; improving the strategic value of the internal audit function; and increased risk monitoring.

The COSO Integrated Framework furthers the goal of optimizing compliance by improving the function's ability to evaluate and improve the internal control environment, which results in a more robust risk management process. This framework sets forth 17 principles, each of which must be present and functioning in an organization for it to have effective internal control. Cyber risk and fraud risk assessment are some critical areas that received expanded guidance. Although the new guidelines were expected to be implemented by the end of 2014, the transition process is still underway for many organizations.

The 2016 global risks report underscores the importance of risk assessment in minimizing the negative impacts of global risks on people, institutions, and economies.[12] The emerging global risks are divided into five general categories of economic, environmental, geopolitical, societal and technological and consist of climate changes in the rising frequency and intensity of water shortages, floods and storms, forcibly displaced people, and crimes in cyberspace cost the global economy an estimated US$445 billion worldwide.[13] Without an enterprise-wide view of risks, an organization is really limiting itself in managing risks and optimizing related compliance to minimize the impacts of emerging global risks. COSO announced in late 2014 a project to update the 2004 Enterprise Risk Management Integrated Framework in reply to the increased importance of enterprise-wide risk assessment and risk management. Both CAEs and audit committee members acknowledged increased concerns about data privacy and security, including cyber risks, which is an area that is addressed with the new COSO framework. To oversee data privacy and security risks, committee members cited steps their board has taken as the following: requesting regular assessments and reporting from management; reviewing policies, procedures, and controls related to data security; and ensuring ongoing monitoring and testing.

In conclusion, CAEs must keep their priorities aligned with their key stakeholders, otherwise the perception and value of the internal audit function will be diminished. By helping stakeholders further their respective goals, internal auditors can improve organizational ability to leverage and optimize compliance activities in pursuit of enterprise-wide risk management priorities. Internal auditors can help their organizations in this respect by improving visibility into financial controls, better allocation of compliance resources, and greater responsiveness to regulatory demands and remediation needs. After helping their organizations to develop a sustainable process for long-term compliance management, internal auditors can then increase their focus on facilitating the value-added operational improvements they view as their next priority.

Cyber Security and Audit Committees

Destructive cyber-attacks such as the Sony Pictures incident (considered the most damaging cyber-attack yet) are outside the norms of cyber practices and can be detrimental to the sustainability of companies.[14] Cyber hacking and security breaches of information systems are becoming a reality for many businesses and threaten their sustainability (e.g., Target, J P Morgan Chase, Home Depot), and their risk assessment and

controls demand significant IT investment and commitment by directors and officers to prevent their occurrence. Sustainability of corporations is significantly affected by the reliability, effectiveness, readiness,
and responsiveness of IT infrastructure and investment. Cybersecurity risk can trigger financial and reputation risks that affect a firm's
bottom-line earnings, as was the case in the recent Sony hack. The cost
of cyber-attacks has exponentially increased in recent years and has been
averaging about $11.6 million per year for firms, about a 78-percent
increase since 2009.[15]

The extent of the audit committee's involvement in cybersecurity
issues varies significantly by company and industry. In one example,
cybersecurity risk is tasked directly to the audit committee, while in
another example, there is a completely separate risk committee. Regardless of the formal structure adopted, audit committees should be aware
of cybersecurity trends, regulatory developments, and major threats to
the company, since the risks associated with intrusions can be severe
and pose systemic economic and business consequences that can significantly affect shareholders. Audit committees should focus on developing and monitoring a cybersecurity plan. Cybersecurity plans should
take into account the past, the present, and the future with regard to
cyber risks. Consideration should be given to what percentage of the
budget should be devoted to prevention efforts, resilience efforts, and
the immediate response to attacks. Cybersecurity activities should extend beyond compliance efforts. A general IT audit is not a replacement
for a full cyber audit.

The National Institute of Standards Technology (NIST) Cybersecurity Framework can help focus the conversation among the senior
management, audit committee, and other member of the board regarding what cybersecurity plans are in place and where there may be gaps.[16]
This framework has been developed through a continuing collaboration
between the government and private industry, and to offer guidance to
assist organizations in voluntarily aligning specific cybersecurity practices. The framework's core consists of five functions—identify, protect, detect, respond, and recover, and related activities that provide
a strategic view of an organization's management of cybersecurity risk
and examine existing cybersecurity practices, guidelines, and standards.

This framework offers a common language by which approaches can be benchmarked across companies and leading practices can be shared.

Conclusion

Enterprise risk management is the keen focus of policymakers, regulators, and businesses in the aftermath of 2007–2009 global financial crisis. Every company, regardless of types and sizes, are subject to financial distress and thus can benefit from adopting. Recent corporate governance reforms (SOX, 2002; Dodd–Frank, 2010) and best practices (COSO, 2004) have required public companies to strengthen their risk assessment and management to prevent further occurrences of global financial crisis. We find that companies that adopt ERM enjoy a short-term decrease in management risk-taking behavior, but the reduced risk-taking behavior disappears in the longer time after the adoption. This chapter suggests that ERM can be more effective and sustainable when it is integrated into corporate governance through creation of either board-level risk committee, risk oversight function of the audit committee, and/or chief risk officer position.

Action Items

1. Oversee the company's ERM system with a keen focus on financial risk.
2. Review and approve the entire ERM strategies, plans, decisions, and actions.
3. Communicate with management, internal auditors, and external auditors the company's ERM as relevant to the financial reporting and audit processes.
4. Periodically (quarterly and annually) review and approve the ERM system.
5. Determine threats that confront company.
6. Estimate the risk, or probability, of each threat occurring.
7. Estimate the exposure, or potential loss, from each threat.
8. Identify set of controls to guard against threat.
9. Estimate costs and benefits from instituting controls.
10. Is it cost beneficial to protect system from threat?
11. Implement set of controls to guard against threat

Endnotes

1. Committee of Sponsoring Organizations (COSO). 2004. Enterprise Risk Management-Integrated Framework. Available at: www.coso.org. For details see APP, *Enterprise Risk Management*.
2. Vedpuiswar, V. 2004. Risk Management at General Motors. Global CEO (January). ICFAI Press.
3. Dodd–Frank Wall Street Reform and Consumer Protection Act. (2010). Available at: http://en.wikipedia.org/wiki/Dodd%E2%80%93Frank_Wall_Street_Reform_and_Consumer_Protection_Act
4. Ibid
5. New York Stock Exchange (NYSE). (2003). Final NYSE corporate governance Rules, NYSE, New York. Available at: www.ecgi.org/codes/documents/finalcorpgovrules.pdf
6. S&P Ratings Direct. (2008). Standard and Poor's to apply enterprise risk analysis to corporate ratings. (May 7, 2008). Standard & Poor's, New York.
7. KPMG's Audit Committee Institute. 2015. Audit Committee Guide. Available at: kpmg.com/ACI
8. Ibid
9. KPMG's Audit Committee Institute. 2015. Calibrating Risk Oversight: Global Boardroom Insights, September 2015. Available at: www.kpmg.com/globalaci
10. PricewaterhouseCoopers. 2007. State of internal audit profession study: Pressures build for continual focus on risk (May). Available at: www.pwc.com/internalaudit
11. Grant Thornton. 2015. Competing Priorities: Are CAE and the Audit Committee Priorities in Sync? Available at: www.grantthorton.com
12. World Economic Forum. 2016. The Global Risks Report 2016, 11th Edition. Available at: www.weforum.org/reports/the-global-risks-report-2016
13. Ibid
14. Banker, P. 2014. U.S. Weights Response to Sony Cyberattack, with North Korea Confrontation Possible. The New York Times. December 18, 2014. Available at www.nytimes.com/2014/12/19/world/asia/north-korea-confrontation-possible-in-response-to-sony-cyberattack.html?_r=0

15. Aguilar, L. A. 2014. Remarks by SEC Commissioner Luis A. Aguilar, "Boards of Directors, Corporate Governance and Cyber-Risks: Sharpening the Focus". June 10, 2014. Available at: www.sec.gov/News/Speech/Detail/Speech/1370542057946#.VEUaY_ldWvg

16. Deloitte. 2015. Risk Intelligent Governance in the Age of Cyber Threats: What You Don't Know Could Hurt You. Available at: www2.deloitte.com/content/dam/Deloitte/global/Documents/Governance-Risk-Compliance/dttl-grc-riskintelligentgovernance intheageofcyberthreats.pdf

CHAPTER 6

Antifraud Oversight Function of the Audit Committee

Executive Summary

Financial reporting fraud (FRF) has been a contributing factor to the recent financial crisis and resulting global economic meltdown, and threatens the efficiency, liquidity, and safety of both debt and capital markets. These threats have significantly increased uncertainty and volatility in financial markets, which has adversely affected investor confidence worldwide. Furthermore, FRF prevents investors from receiving meaningful financial information to make savvy investment decisions. Thus, effective corporate governance in promoting antifraud policies and practices is necessary to prevent this phenomenon. This chapter examines the effectiveness of the established antifraud policies and practices in preventing and detecting FRF and the oversight function of the audit committee in reducing incidents of FRF.

Introduction

High quality of financial information is the lifeblood of the capital markets and that quality can be adversely affected by the existence and persistence of FRF, which is a severe threat to investor confidence in financial information and thus capital markets. The recent subprime loan mortgage crisis and resulting economic downturn have also provided incentives and opportunities for management to engage in FRF. When the company is not effective in generating sustainable performance, management is under more pressure to manage earnings.

Opportunities to engage in FRF are higher when the company is not doing well financially and is unable to invest in effective corporate governance and internal controls in designing and maintaining proper antifraud policies and practices. Emerging corporate governance reforms, security laws, and best practices are intended to identify and minimize potential conflicts of interest, incentives, and opportunities to engage in FRF.

Corporate governance has garnered considerable attention in the wake of the recent global financial crisis and is now emerging as a central issue for regulators and public companies. Large public companies have recently undergone a series of regulatory reforms resulting from legislation imposed by the U.S. Congress (e.g., Sarbanes–Oxley Act of 2002 [SOX], Dodd–Frank Act of 2010).[1] In particular, corporate governance measures including proper antifraud policies and practices are intended to protect investors from receiving fraudulent financial information. Thus, effective corporate governance in strengthening antifraud policies and practices promotes accountability, improves the reliability and quality of financial information, enhances the integrity and efficiency of the capital market, and improves investor confidence. Poor corporate governance adversely affects the company's potential, performance, financial reports, and accountability and can pave the way for business failure, fraudulent public financial information, inefficiency in capital markets, and loss of investor confidence.

One of the key responsibilities of corporate governance participants is to ensure the quality, integrity, reliability, and transparency of financial statements and provide a reasonable assurance that they are free from any misstatements caused by errors or fraud. Proper antifraud policies and practices improve the effectiveness of corporate governance and thus reliability of financial statements. Antifraud policies and practices are classified into preventing, detecting, and correcting corporate governance measures influenced by all corporate gatekeepers including the board of directors including the audit committee, management, internal auditors, and external auditors. Effective fulfillment of antifraud roles and responsibilities of corporate gatekeepers is expected to prevent, detect, and correct FRF, and thus prevent occurrences of the 2007–2008 global financial crisis.

Antifraud Policies and Practices

Corporate governance measures are designed to protect shareholders and other stakeholders' interests by limiting opportunistic behavior of managers who control their interests. In particular, corporate governance measures including proper antifraud policies and practices are intended to protect investors from receiving fraudulent financial information. Thus, effective corporate governance in strengthening antifraud policies and practices promotes accountability, improves the reliability and quality of financial information, enhances the integrity and efficiency of the capital market, and improves investor confidence. Poor corporate governance adversely affects the company's potential, performance, financial reports, and accountability and can pave the way for business failure, fraudulent public financial information, inefficiency in capital markets, and loss of investor confidence. One of the key responsibilities of corporate governance participants is to ensure the quality, integrity, reliability, and transparency of financial statements and provide a reasonable assurance that they are free from any misstatements caused by errors or fraud. Proper antifraud policies and practices improve the effectiveness of corporate governance and thus reliability of financial statements.

The existence and persistence of FRF is harmful in many ways by undermining the quality and integrity of the financial reporting process, diminishing investor confidence in the reliability of financial information, causing the capital market to be less efficient, destroying the careers of individuals involved in FRF, causing bankruptcy or substantial economic losses by the company engaged in FRF, encouraging excessive regulatory intervention, and causing destructions in the normal operations and performance of alleged companies.[2] Antifraud policies and practices as described in Exhibit 6.1 can prevent and detect FRF. These antifraud policies and practices are classified into preventing, detecting, and correcting corporate governance measures influenced by all corporate gatekeepers including the board of directors that includes the audit committee, management, internal auditors, and external auditors. The board of directors and its audit committee as representative of all stakeholders (investors, employees, society) has a fiduciary duty to protect their interests and ensure that their decisions (investment, employment) are not affected by misleading financial information. The effectiveness of the board oversight function depends on directors' independence, due process, authority, resources, composition, qualifications, and accountability. Senior executives consisting of the chief executive officer (CEO) and chief financial officer (CFO) are responsible for managing the company and its resources and operations as well as certifying the accuracy and completeness of financial reports. The effectiveness of the managerial function depends on the alignment of management's interests with those of shareholders and ensuring reliability of financial reports. Internal auditors are regarded as the first defense against fraudulent activities providing both assurance and consulting services to the company in the areas of operational efficiency, risk management, internal controls, financial reporting, antifraud, and governance processes. Auditing standards (SAS Nos 88 and 99, 2002) require that external auditors provide *reasonable assurance* that the financial statements are free from material misstatements, whether caused by error or fraud.[3]

Exhibit 6.1

Antifraud mechanisms

Prevention mechanisms	Detection mechanisms	Correction mechanisms
1. Vigilant board of directors	1. Adequate and effective internal control structure	1. Restatement of current year fraudulent financial statements
2. Vigilant audit committee	2. Responsible legal counsel	2. Restatement of current and prior years' fraudulent financial statements
3. Diligent management	3. Alert, skeptical external audit assurance function	3. Ramification of motives and opportunities contributed to the commission of financial reporting fraud
4. Adequate and effective internal audit function	4. External regulatory oversight procedure	4. Establishment and implementation of strategies to regain public confidence in the integrity, quality, and reliability of financial reports

Since the passage of the SOX of July 2002, which was intended to combat financial fraud, the Department of Justice has prosecuted 1,300 fraud convictions.[4] The 2007 subprime loan mortgage crisis and resulting economic downturn also provide incentives and opportunities for management to engage in FRF.[5] The 2010 COSO report finds 347 cases of FRF during 1998–2007 compared with 294 fraud incidents during 1987–1997.When the company is not effective in generating sustainable performance, management is under more pressure to manage earnings.[6] Opportunities to engage in FRF are higher when the company is not doing well financially and unable to invest in effective corporate governance and internal controls in designing and maintaining proper antifraud policies and practices. Emerging corporate governance reforms, securities laws, and best practices are intended to identify and minimize potential conflicts of interest, incentives, and opportunities to engage in FRF. Financial reporting fraud has been a contributing factor to the recent financial crisis and resulting global economic meltdown and threatens the efficiency, liquidity, and safety of both debt and capital markets. These threats have significantly increased uncertainty and volatility in financial markets, which has adversely affected investor confidence worldwide. Furthermore, FRF prevents investors from receiving meaningful financial information to make savvy investment decisions. Thus, effective corporate governance in promoting antifraud policies and practices is necessary to prevent this phenomenon.

The Audit Committee Role in Preventing and Detecting Fraud

Antifraud roles, responsibilities, policies, and practices of corporate governance gatekeepers including the board of directors, the audit committee, external auditors, and internal auditors are more important than ever. While executive management including legal counsel and human resources has the primary responsibility for the antifraud efforts of the company, the corporate gatekeepers oversee and support management. In the context of fraud, corporate gatekeepers' roles and responsibilities are to deter, prevent, detect, investigate, and remediate fraud, defined as any intentional wrongful acts to deceive, mislead, and harm from theft of assets to FRF.

High-profile FRF cases such as Enron, WorldCom, Adelphia, and more recently, Madoff, Satyam, and Stanford Financial have raised serious concerns about: (1) the role of corporate gatekeepers in preventing, detecting, and remediating fraud; and (2) the integrity, competency, and ethical reporting practices of management; (3) the ineffectiveness of audit functions in detecting and reporting fraud; and (4) the important role that corporate legal counsel plays in compliance with applicable laws, rules, and regulations.

The audit committee should oversee management's efforts to establish and implement antifraud programs and controls. The audit committee has oversight responsibilities for the company's antifraud programs, activities, and controls designed to prevent and detect fraud in general and financial statement fraud in particular. SAS No. 99 requires auditors to plan and perform the financial audit to obtain reasonable assurance that financial statements are free of material misstatements, whether caused by error or fraud.[7] SAS No. 99 does not specify any model that can be used by the auditor in assessing the risk of material misstatements due to fraud. The ownership structure (debt vs. equity), corporate governance characteristics (e.g., audit committee effectiveness), financial attributes (e.g., earnings quality), size, and complexity of the audit client's organization have a significant effect on the identification of relevant fraud risk factors. The auditor should communicate with the audit committee all matters involving fraud regardless of their materiality.

The auditor should ask management to revise financial statements to correct misstatements caused by fraud or otherwise express a qualified or an adverse opinion. Auditors should consider fraud risk factors relevant to: (1) misstatements arising from fraudulent financial reporting; and (2) misstatements arising from misappropriation of assets. These fraud risk factors should be evaluated and used in modifying the nature, timing, and extent of audit procedures to be performed in detecting fraud. Auditors should also communicate these fraud risk factors with the audit committee. The board of directors and its audit committee is the ultimate gatekeeper and control mechanism whose responsibility is to protect the interests of stakeholders. The board of directors should have a written protocol that outlines its response when allegations of unethical behavior, fraud, and other corporate malfeasance come to light. Further, according to "Managing the Business Risk of Fraud: A Practical Guide," the following summarizes the roles and responsibilities of the board of directors with regard to fraud:

- Set the appropriate tone at the top
- Make fraud prevention, deterrence, and detection a periodic agenda item
- Maintain control over the sources and the flow of information it needs to complete its work
- Maintain access to management and employees, financial and operational personnel
- Encourage ethical behavioral and act accordingly
- Empower (create expectations) for employees, customers, vendors, and so on with regard to ethics and fraud
- Understand fraud risks
- Monitor management's:
  - Risk assessments
  - Antifraud policies and control (prevention and deterrence)
  - Assurance that controls are effective to ensure timely and accurate reporting (detection, investigation, and remediation)
- Retain and compensate outside expertise when necessary
- Provide external auditors with evidence of the board of directors' commitment to and involvement in fraud risk management.

Deloitte and Touche suggests that the audit committee should oversee management antifraud activities regarding: (1) fraud risk assessment; (2) the antifraud control environment; (3) antifraud programs and control activities; (4) communicating and sharing information; and (5) monitoring activities.[8]

Assessing Fraud Risk

Management is primarily responsible for performing fraud risk assessments on a continuous basis to identify factors or events that could cause fraud to occur. The audit committee should oversee management's fraud risk assessment and obtain an understanding of risk factors and events such as related-party transactions and improper revenue recognition that threaten the integrity and reliability of financial statements.

Establishing an Antifraud Control Environment

The company's control environment, management philosophy, operating style, corporate governance, culture, and ethical values all play an important role in creating an environment that prevents occurrences of fraud. Management is responsible for establishing an antifraud control environment to address: (1) financial statement fraud, including manipulation of financial statements; (2) misappropriation of assets; (3) illegal acts and corruption; (4) employee fraud; and (5) other fraud-related matters. The audit committee should oversee management efforts in establishing an antifraud control environment.

Design and Operation of Antifraud Programs and Control Activities

Besides establishing the proper environment, management also must establish adequate and effective antifraud programs and control activities to prevent, detect, and correct fraudulent financial activities. The audit committee should oversee the adequacy and effectiveness of antifraud control activities and understand the nature and scope of antifraud programs.

Communicating and Sharing Information

To achieve their intended objectives, the company's antifraud programs must be communicated throughout the company. Management must ensure that all personnel adequately understand the company's code of conduct and antifraud programs and activities designed to prevent, detect, and correct misconduct, unethical behavior, and fraudulent activities. The audit committee should oversee the existence of the company's code of ethics and antifraud programs and ascertain that they effectively have been communicated to all personnel within the company. The audit committee should also establish an appropriate whistle-blower program to facilitate and encourage employees to report to the audit committee any allegations of improper or unethical conduct and fraudulent activities. Next Chapter discusses in depth the whistle-blower oversight responsibilities of the audit committee.

Monitoring Antifraud Programs and Control Activities

The established and communicated antifraud programs and control activities should be monitored continuously to ensure their enforcement and compliance by all personnel within the company. Management, assisted by internal auditors, should assess the effectiveness of the design, implementation, and compliance with antifraud programs and control activities. The audit committee should monitor management's and internal audit's activities relevant to risk assessment and antifraud programs.

In summary, the audit committee is responsible for overseeing the company's risk assessment and enterprise risk management, particularly risks relevant to financial reporting. Management and the internal auditor should inform the audit committee of significant risk threatening the integrity, reliability, and quality of financial reports. The audit committee should oversee the company's enterprise risk management including risks associated with operations, financial reporting, management misconduct, conflicts of interest, trading securities (insider trading, fraud), related-party transactions, assets misappropriations, travel and entertainment, and executive compensation expenses. The audit committee should ask management to list potential risks in terms of importance and their effects on the company's operations and financial reports. The audit committee should be assured that management establish and maintain adequate and effective internal controls to manage risks. The audit committee should work with management, internal and external auditors, and legal counsel in developing and implementing antifraud policies and practices that focus on setting a tone at the top promoting ethical and competent culture throughout the organization, advocate professional skepticism and practices, and mobilize an integrated approach and full engagement and participation by everyone in the organization in combating fraud.

Antifraud Roles and Responsibilities of External Auditors

External auditors provide a reasonable assurance that financial statements are free from material misstatements caused by errors and fraud. Auditors increase the perception of detection as well as the likelihood of catching fraudsters. The following can be used by professionals in their interaction with auditors to ensure that the auditor's efforts with regard to fraud detection will help reduce the risk of undetected fraud.

- Examine traditional internal controls that mitigate the risk of fraud including:
  - reconciliations
  - independent internal reviews
  - appropriate approvals
  - conduct independent physical inspections, periodic inventory counts,
  - confirm transaction details with outside participants
  - complete performance analysis and compliance testing.
- Be unpredictable.
- Incorporate proactive fraud detection procedures in areas with high probabilities of fraud occurrence and significant dollar magnitude
- Investigate anomalies (e.g., red flags), unexpected trends, and suspicious journal entries.
- Utilize data extraction and analysis, also called data mining, tools to proactively search for fraud
- Proactively search for symptoms of collusion and management override:
  - Review journal entries
  - Review of estimates
  - Review of unusual/significant (non-recurring) transactions
- Examine management's documentation of their written detection protocols with respect to fraud prevention, deterrence, and detection:
  - Overall fraud detection process

- ○ Specific fraud detection controls
- ○ The implementation of those controls
- ○ How management approaches continuous improvement: assessing and updating the design and implementation of deterrence and detection tools and techniques
- Auditors may also want to examine management reports of the performance of their clients' antifraud efforts, paying particular attention to the following:
- ○ Recurring frauds
- ○ Losses and the value associated with by preventing future (similar) frauds
- ○ The timeliness of design changes/improvements in fraud prevention, deterrence, and detection activities

Antifraud Roles and Responsibilities of Internal Auditors

The following are key characteristics of an effective antifraud internal audit group:

- Reports to the Audit Committee or in such a manner so as to be considered independent of management.
- Is properly trained and professionally qualified in fraud risk assessment, fraud schemes and fraud prevention, deterrence and detection.
- Has sufficient knowledge, training, and experience with regard to the red flag symptoms of fraud schemes.
- Has a commitment to design audit plans based on fraud risk assessments.
- Uses brainstorming techniques as part of risk assessment.
- Is professionally skeptical.
- Is unpredictable.
- Responds to concerns over allegations and suspicions of collusive behaviors and management override.
- Is committed to evidence-based decision-making, including the use of nonfinancial data and information.

Internal audit's antifraud roles and responsibilities can be carried out in the following areas:

- Provide a critical evaluation of the organization's antifraud measures
- Assess the organization's culture
- Conduct surveys to measure the organization's ethical environment
- Assess fraud detection activities
- Let the board of directors, audit committee, senior management, managers, supervisors, and line employees and staff know that internal audit is:
  - Looking for fraud
  - Welcomes tips, complaints, allegation and information regarding suspicions of fraud
  - Asks tough questions of management and employees
  - Conducts timely investigations of allegations and suspicions of fraud acts, including those associated with collusive behavior and management override
- Internal audit should examine whistle-blower hotlines and other reporting mechanisms:
  - Multilingual
  - 24/7 availability
  - Genuine anonymity
  - No retaliation or retribution against persons who report concerns
  - Appropriate and timely reaction to the concerns of those reporting
  - Existence and availability of the hotline is communicated to employees, customers, vendors, and suppliers
  - Hotline personnel have a protocol for who is notified: manager/supervisor, senior management, audit committee, legal, human resources, ethics/ compliance officer, security.

Conclusion

Organizations of all sizes are susceptible to both employee (theft, embezzlement) and management fraud (manipulating financial reports) in creating misleading financial reports. Effective antifraud policies and programs should be designed by the audit committee to prevent and detect fraud. Antifraud programs should deter, prevent, and detect all variations of fraud, from misrepresenting financial information to misappropriating assets and employee fraud. Effective antifraud programs should also address the antifraud role of corporate governance participants. Corporate governance has evolved as a central issue within regulators and public companies in wake of the recent global financial crisis. Companies have recently undergone a series of corporate governance reforms aimed at improving the effectiveness of their governance, internal controls, and financial reports. Effective corporate governance promotes accountability, improves the reliability and quality of financial information, and prevents financial reporting fraud. Poor corporate governance adversely affects the company's potential, performance, financial reports, and accountability, and can pave the way for business failure and financial reporting fraud. Corporate governance measures of the oversight function assumed by the board of directors, managerial function delegated to management, internal audit function conducted by internal auditors, and external audit function performed by external auditors are vital to the quality of financial information. All corporate gatekeepers including the board of directors, the audit committee, internal and external auditors play an important role in preventing detecting and correcting FRF. The invaluable role of corporate governance in a firm's antifraud efforts is paramount to success. The insights and tips should help ensure that corporate governance is operating at the highest level of antifraud competency.

Action Items

1. Establish corporate antifraud policies and practices including fraud deterrence, prevention, detection, and investigation and remediation mechanisms.
2. Create an appropriate corporate culture and environment that promotes competent, ethical behavior, reinforces antifraud conduct, and demands that corporate participants do the right thing.
3. Design control structure that minimizes or eliminates opportunities for individuals to engage in fraudulent activities and ensures early fraud detection.

4. Establish antifraud procedures to react to and remediate allegations of fraud.

5. Employ forensic accounting consultants to conduct investigations in discovering allegations of FRF.

6. Engage the incumbent audit firm to conduct fraud investigation.

Endnotes

1. Sarbanes-Oxley Act. 2002. 107 Congress, 2nd session. PL 107-204, HR 3763 (July 24, 2002), Dodd-Frank Wall Street Reform and Consumer Protection Act (the "Act") 2010.

2. Rezaee, Z., & Riley, R. 2009. *Financial Reporting Fraud: Prevention and Detection* (2nd ed.). Hoboken, NJ: John Wiley & Sons.

3. American Institute of Certified Public Accountants (AICPA). *Statement on Auditing Standards No. 82, Consideration of Fraud in a Financial Statement Audit.* AICPA: New York, NY; and American Institute of Certified Public Accountants (AICPA). 2002. Consideration of fraud in a financial statement audit. *Statement on Auditing Standards No. 99.* New York, NY: AICPA.

4. Mark Philip, "Message from the Chairman," 2008 Report to the President: Corporate Fraud Task Force. Available at: www .usdoj.gov/dag/cftf/corporate-fraud2008.pdf

5. Rezaee, Z., & Riley, R. 2009. *Financial Reporting Fraud: Prevention and Detection* (2nd ed.). Hoboken, NJ: John Wiley & Sons.

6. Committee of Sponsoring Organizations of the Treadway Commission (COSO). 2010. Fraudulent Financial Reporting: 1998–2007: An Analysis of U.S. Public Companies. Available at: www.coso.org

7. American Institute of Certified Public Accountants (AICPA). 2002. Statement on Auditing Standards (SAS) No. 99. Consideration of Fraud in Financial Statements Audit. Available at: www.aicpa.org

8. Deloitte & Touche. 2004. Fraud and the Role of the Audit Committee. Audit Committee Brief, Special Edition (June). Available at: www.auditcommittee.com/

CHAPTER 7

Ethics and Compliance Oversight Function of the Audit Committee

Executive Summary

It takes only a few unfavorable incidents (the 2001 Enron debacle and the 2007–2009 global financial crisis) to significantly erode public trust and investor confidence in public financial information and financial markets. It requires an enormous effort by policymakers, regulators, professional organizations, and public companies to restore embattled public trust and investor confidence. The wave of financial scandals in the early 2000s, the 2007–2009 global financial crisis, and subsequent regulatory responses have galvanized considerable ethics and compliance oversight function of the audit committee as explained in this chapter. The audit committee should review and approve the company's code of business conduct and compliance process and ensure compliance with both the code and compliance programs.

Introduction

The current financial crisis was partially caused by a number of ethical lapses made by organizations and individuals involved in the mortgage markets, including mortgage originators, financial intermediaries, and mortgage borrowers. The crisis and related financial scandals have policymakers, regulators, and ethics advocates questioning how business is normally conducted and to what extent ethics and corporate culture affect the business process and whether ethics performance should be reflected in overall corporate reporting. Professional ethics is a set of moral principles, best practices, and standards that guide business and professional behavior. Professional ethics refers to the collective values of business and professional organizations that can be used to evaluate whether the behavior of the collective members of the organization is considered acceptable and appropriate and whether businesses and professionals are held accountable for their openness, integrity, and ethical behavior.

Ethics and Ethical Principles

The wave of financial scandals, financial crisis, and related regulatory responses and best practices have galvanized demand for and interest in ethics and compliance training programs. Ethics is broadly described in the literature as moral principles about right and wrong, honorable behavior reflecting values, or standards of conduct.[1] Honesty, openness, responsiveness, accountability, due diligence, and fairness are the core ethical principles. Professional ethics is a specialized study of moral right and wrong, using appropriate professional judgment, and being accountable for ethical decisions and actions. An appropriate code of ethics that sets the right tone at the top of promoting ethical and professional conduct and establishing the moral structure for the entire organization is the backbone of effective corporate governance.

Section 406 of Sarbanes–Oxley Act of 2002 (SOX) and Securities and Exchange Commission (SEC)–elated rules require that the following: (1) all public companies adhere to the Exchange Act reporting requirements except registered investment companies that must disclose whether they have adopted a written code of ethics for principal executive, financial, or accounting officers, controllers, or persons performing similar functions; (2) if they have not, explain why not; and (3) subject companies to promptly disclose amendments to and waivers from codes of ethics for any of those officers.[2] The SEC rule defines a code of ethics as a written standard designed to deter wrongdoing and to promote: (1) ethical and honest conduct; (2) professional resolution of actual or apparent conflicts of interest between personal and professional relationships; (3) fair, full, timely, and transparent disclosures in financial reporting; (4) compliance with applicable laws, regulations, rules, and standards; (5) accountability for adherence to the code; and (6) to promote reporting of code violations to appropriate internal parties identified in the code.[3] Public companies must include their code of ethics disclosure in their annual reports filed with the Commission and make their code of ethics publicly available through (1) filing a copy with the SEC as an exhibit to their annual report; (2) posting the text of their code of ethics on their website; and (3) indicating in their annual reports that they will provide a copy of their code of ethics to any person upon request without charge.

Companies should set the appropriate "tone at the top" in promoting and enforcing ethical conduct throughout the organization. To foster ethical conduct, many companies in recent years have appointed a "chief ethics officer" who functionally reports to the audit committee and administratively to the CEO. The audit committee, the chief ethics officer, and the chief audit executive (CAE) should work closely to establish ethics policies, communicate them to employees, maintain compliance, investigate noncompliance, report results, and recommend ways to prevent further occurrence of ethics violations. This section discusses the ethics oversight function of the audit committee.

Codes of Business Conduct

The Treadway Commission suggests that the most important factor in preventing fraudulent financial reporting is a company's "tone at the top" promoting ethical conduct.[4] The company's board of directors and audit committee must set a proper tone at the top by promoting, encouraging, and enforcing ethical conduct and compliance with applicable laws and regulations. The Treadway Commission recommends that all public companies establish written codes of conduct providing—at a minimum—guidelines regarding: (1) conflicts of interest; (2) compliance with applicable laws and regulations, both domestic and foreign; and (3) confidentiality of proprietary information.[5]

The listing standards of the NYSE state that each company "may determine its own policies" while providing a fairly extensive listing of important matters that the code of business conduct should address including: (1) the resolution of conflicts of interest; (2) corporate opportunities; (3) confidentiality; (4) fair dealing with the company's competitors, employees, customers, suppliers, and other stakeholders; (5) protection and proper use of company assets; (6) compliance with laws, rules, and regulations; and (7) facilitating the reporting of any illegal or unethical behavior.[6]

SOX provisions and SEC final rules are basically disclosure requirements in the sense that companies that have not adopted codes of ethics must disclose this and explain why. The SEC rules and listing standards should be incorporated into the company's overall business codes of conduct for the entire company and its personnel. The company's overall codes of business conduct should (1) set an appropriate tone at the top promoting ethical and honest conduct for all its personnel; (2) establish policies and procedures for appropriate and timely resolutions of actual and apparent conflicts of interest between its personnel; (3) promote and require fair, full, transparent, and accurate disclosures in its external financial reports, particularly those filed with the SEC and other public disclosures; (4) require compliance with applicable laws, rules, regulations, and standards; (5) design enforceable procedures for compliance with the established codes of business ethics; (6) provide internal reporting mechanisms for reporting and consideration of violations of ethics policies and procedures by appropriate authorities within the company; (7) hold all personnel accountable for compliance with the code; (8) establish a review process to ensure the company's code of ethics continues to align with the emerging corporate governance reforms; (9) combine the code of ethics in compliance with SEC rules with codes of conduct required by the listing standards of national stock exchanges (NYSE, NASDAQ), and other applicable or regulatory codes of ethics, and (10) make the company code of ethics publicly available by either posting it on the company's website and disclosing the address in the annual report or include it as an exhibit in the annual report.

Establishing Codes of Business Conduct

Rezaee and Lander (1993: 39) state that, "Establishing codes of business conduct is not an easy task because ethics in its truest meaning cannot be reduced to standards. Ethics is a mental concept and a part of morals, which can be neither totally written nor legislated."[7] Nevertheless, in the post-SOX era, the company's audit committee should oversee the establishment, implementation, enforcement, and monitoring of codes of conduct. If a company does not have a code of business conduct in compliance with the provisions of SOX, the audit committee should establish an ethics committee consisting of senior officers of human resources, internal audit function, all major departments, and legal counsel. This ethics committee prepares the company's code of business conduct in compliance with the requirements of SOX, listing standards, or other applicable guidelines.

The proposed code of business conduct should be reviewed by the audit committee and submitted to the company's board of directors for final approval. The approved code of business conduct should be distributed to all employees, properly implemented, and monitored. The audit committee should require that the company's internal audit function be responsible for enforcement and monitoring of the code of business conduct by obtaining certification from employees, particularly those in key financial positions, including senior executives (CEO, CFO). Employees should certify that they are not aware of any non-adherence to the code personally or of any violations by personnel reporting to them. Any significant infraction should be investigated by the internal auditor, reported to the ethics committee, and reviewed by the audit committee.

A code of ethics is a set of written standards that are reasonably designed to deter wrongdoing and to promote:

1. Honest and ethical conduct, including the ethical handling of actual or apparent conflicts of interest between personal and professional relationships;
2. Avoidance of conflicts of interest, including disclosure to an appropriate person or persons identified in the code of any material transaction or relationship that reasonably could be expected to give rise to such a conflict;
3. Full, fair, accurate, timely, and transparent disclosure in reports and documents that a company files with, or submits to, the SEC and in other public communications made by the company;
4. Compliance with applicable laws, rules, regulations, and standards;
5. The prompt internal reporting to an appropriate person or persons identified in the code of violations of the code;

6. Accountability for adherence to the code.
7. Safeguarding the proper use of the company's assets.
8. Fair dealing with the company's investors, creditors, competitors, customers, suppliers, employees, and other stakeholders.

Exhibit 7.1 shows the Coca-Cola Company's code of business conduct. This code of business conduct is very specific and addresses the administration of the code including responsibility, investigation of potential code violations, decisions, disciplinary actions, reporting of

Exhibit 7.1

Condensed Coca-Cola code of business conduct

Administration of the code

The Code of Business Conduct is designed to ensure consistency in how employees conduct themselves within the Company, and in their dealings outside of the Company. The procedures for handling potential violations of the Code have been developed to ensure consistency in the process across the organization.

Responsibility

The responsibility for administering the Code rests with the Ethics & Compliance Committee, which is comprised of senior leaders representing corporate governance functions as well as operations.

Investigation of potential code violations

The Company takes all reports of potential Code violations seriously and is committed to confidentiality and a full investigation of all allegations. The Company's Audit, Finance, Legal, Ethics & Compliance, and Strategic Security personnel may conduct or manage Code investigations. Employees who are being investigated for a potential Code violation will have an opportunity to be heard prior to any final determination. The Company follows local grievance procedures in locations where such procedures apply.

Decisions

The Ethics & Compliance Committee makes all decisions about Code violations and discipline, but may delegate certain categories of decision to local management. Those found to have violated the Code can seek reconsideration of the violation and disciplinary action decisions.

Disciplinary actions

The Company strives to impose discipline that fits the nature and circumstances of each Code violation. Violations of a serious nature may result in suspension without pay; loss or reduction of merit increase, bonus or stock option award; or termination of employment.

Reporting of code decisions and investigations

The Ethics & Compliance Office periodically reports all pending Code investigations and final Code decisions, including disciplinary actions taken, to senior management of the Company and to the Audit Committee of the Board of Directors. The Ethics & Compliance Office also posts a representative sample of Code violations, with personal identifying characteristics removed, on the Ethics & Compliance intranet site for the education of employees.

Signature and acknowledgment

All new employees must sign an acknowledgment form confirming that they have read the Code of Business Conduct and agree to abide by its provisions. All employees will be required to make similar acknowledgments on a periodic basis. Failure to read the Code or sign the acknowledgment form does not excuse an employee from compliance with the Code.

Waivers

Waivers of any provisions of this Code for officers of the Company must be approved by the Board of Directors or its designated committee and will be disclosed promptly to the extent required by law.

Source: Adapted from Coca-Cola Code of Business Conduct. Available at: www2.coca-cola. com/ourcompany/pdf/business_conduct_codes.pdf

code decisions and investigations, signature and acknowledgment, and waivers. The company's directors, officers, and employees receive a copy of the code of business conduct, which is already approved by principal managers, requires reporting of code violations directly to the ethics and compliance officer, requires investigation of such violations by the general counsel and chief financial officer, and finally imposes discipline for each code violation including suspension without pay, loss or reduction of merit increase, bonus, or stock option awards, or termination of employment.

Exhibit 7.2 presents General Motors' (GM) vision statement consisting of core values, personal integrity, and integrity in the workplace (including the integrity of financial reports, integrity in the marketplace, and integrity in society and communities). GM's vision statement promotes ethical conduct throughout the company. GM's vision of being the world leader in transportation products and services is guided by its core values. GM's core values are customer enthusiasm, continuous improvement, integrity, teamwork, innovation, and individual respect and responsibility. GM's cultural priorities consist of enhancing product and customer focus, acting as one company, embracing stretch targets, and moving with a sense of urgency.

Exhibit 7.2
Condensed General Motor's code of ethics outline

Vision statement

GM's vision is to be the world leader in transportation products and related services. We will earn our customers' enthusiasm through continuous improvement driven by the integrity, teamwork, and innovation of GM people.

Core values

Core values consist of: (1) customer enthusiasm; (2) continuous improvement; (3) integrity; (4) teamwork; (5) innovation; and (6) individual respect and responsibility.

Cultural priorities

Cultural priorities consist of: (1) enhancing product and customer focus; (2) acting as one company; (3) embracing stretch targets; and (4) moving with a sense of urgency.

I. Personal Integrity

II. Integrity in the Workplace

  (a) Fair Treatment and Respect

We hire, promote, train, and pay based on merit, experience, or other work-related criteria.

  (b) Equal Employment Opportunity

GM is committed to equal employment opportunity.

  (c) Speak Up for Safety

At General Motors, we have an obligation to provide a safe work environment for every employee, contractor, and visitor at every GM location.

  (d) Conflicts of Interest

Your disclosure of a potential conflict provides your management with information to clarify potential conflicts and resolve as appropriate.

  (e) Protection and Use of GM Information and Resources

      I. Accuracy of Business Records

     II. Personal Information and Privacy Concerns

    III. Information Lifecycle Management

    IV. Litigation and Investigations

     V. Communicating With the Media

III. Integrity in the Marketplace

  (a) Giving To and Receiving From Third Parties (including Government Officials)

  (b) Fair Competition

  (c) Insider Trading

  (d) Export Compliance

IV. Integrity Toward the Environment

  (a) GM Environmental Principles

  (b) Dangerous Goods in Transportation

Source: Adapted from General Motors. *Winning with Integrity: Our Values and Guidelines for Employee Conduct.* Available at: www.gm.com/content/dam/gmcom/COMPANY/Investors/ Corporate_Governance/PDFs/WWI.pdf

A well-established and effectively enforced code of conduct provides ethical standards and guidelines on resolution of conflicts of interest, compliance with applicable laws, rules and regulations, confidentiality and proprietary of information, and fair dealing with investors, customers, suppliers, employees, and other interested parties. The emerging corporate governance reforms require that the audit committee oversee the establishment of the company's code of business conduct, proper communication to all personnel, enforcement of compliance with the code, investigation of any noncompliance, implementation of disciplinary actions, and proper reporting and disclosure of any violations.

Ethics in Practice

An online poll conducted in January 2005 by the Dallas chapter of the International Association of Business Communicators (Dallas/IABC) reveals that (1) about 30 percent of respondents indicate that they have been asked to compromise their integrity often, very often, or extremely often; (2) more than 10 percent responded that they have been asked to compromise their integrity extremely often; and (3) the remaining 69 percent said they have never or not often been asked by management to compromise their integrity.[8] Those results suggest that employees and even executives are still under pressure to compromise their integrity despite the requirements of emerging corporate governance reforms (SOX, listing standards) for the establishment of a code of business ethics for senior executives and employees that promotes ethical conduct by setting a "right tone at the top." The audit committee should promote an ethical work environment free of pressures or incentives for senior executives and other employees to compromise their integrity and professional responsibility. Factors that can promote ethical workplace are:

1. Management behavior (Tone at the Top).
2. Behavior of Peers.
3. Rewarding good behavior.
4. Punishing bad behavior.

Reasons for making unethical decisions are:

1. Lack of clear ethical guidance and ineffective enforcement.
2. Job dissatisfaction.
3. Pressure to achieve unattainable goals.
4. Lack of personal integrity.
5. Ignorance of codes of conduct.
6. Lack of accountability.
7. The misconception that if "everybody else is doing it" it has to be ethical.

Ethics and Compliance Reporting

The audit committee in collaboration with senior management and the internal audit department should design the business code of conduct, ensure communication of the code to all directors, officers, and employees, seek certification of compliance with the code, and require ethics reporting consisting of the following items:

- Existence of ethics-related board committee or chief ethics executive position
- Establishment, maintenance, and enforcement codes of ethical conduct.
- Development of ethics program, policies, and procedures.
- Communication, implementation, and certification of compliance with the established ethics policies and procedures.
- Compliance with all applicable laws, rules, regulations, standards, and best practices.
- Adoption of internal mechanisms for resolution of unethical dilemmas to minimize their existence and persistence.
- Integration of whistle-blowing policies into ethics programs and practices to institutionalize ethics in the workplace.
- Existence of administrative and training of ethics policies and procedures to internally resolve ethics dilemmas and conflicts of interest.

- Development of grievance policies and procedures to internally resolve any disagreements and disputes with supervisors and staff
- Establishment of an ethics hotline or an anonymous suggestion box in which personnel are enabled to report internally suspected unethical activities.
- Statement of policy for anti-discrimination based on race, color, ethnicity, gender, and religion.
- Mechanisms to ensure minimal pressure, incentives, and opportunities for employees to compromise their professional responsibilities and ethical standards.
- Emphasis on customer relations to enhance the company's reputation.
- Encouragement of whistle-blowers to reveal dishonesty and wrongdoings.
- Control structure eliminates opportunities for individuals to engage in unethical activities.

Assurance on Ethics Reports

Credibility, objectivity, and reliability of ethics reports can be significantly enhanced by providing assurance for these reports. Internal auditors should provide the audit committee with an ethics assurance reporting containing proper answers to the following questions:

- Does the company have ethics committee at the board level or officer position?
- Does the company maintain effective codes of conduct and ethics standards?
- Does the company maintain effective whistle-blowing policies and procedures?
- Do employees' actions comply with the spirit and letter of all applicable laws, rules, regulations, and standards?
- Is personnel behavior consistent with the company's core values and ethical standards?
- Are there mechanisms for providing incentives and opportunities to behave ethically and do the right thing?

- Are there policies and procedures for hiring the most competent and ethical personnel?
- Are there proper mechanisms for effective resolution of conflicts of interest?

Whistle-Blower Oversight Function

A review of headline-making financial scandals reveals that in many cases internal staff, internal auditors, and financial analysts voiced concerns regarding accounting, financial reporting, internal controls, or auditing matters of those companies. However, there generally existed no formal whistle-blower programs or complaint mechanisms for individuals concerned to take proper actions to report wrongdoings to authorities or persons in a position to prevent and correct wrongdoings. SOX created the opportunity for confidential and anonymous submissions of complaints by requiring the company's audit committee to establish procedures for the receipt, retention, and treatment of such complaints.[9]

The SOX of 2002 and SEC-related rules require that the audit committee establish and maintain appropriate whistle-blower programs for the receipt, process, and retention of complaints regarding internal control accounting and auditing matters.[10] Such programs must establish procedures and mechanisms that encompass the confidential and anonymous submission of concerns on questionable accounting and auditing matters by employees. The SEC requires that the audit committee establish specific mechanisms tailored and suitable to the company's circumstances and needs for whistle-blower programs. The whistle-blowing program must be established in compliance with both the SOX of 2002 and the Dodd–Frank Act (DOF) of 2010. Section 301 of the SOX contain whistle-blowing provisions that require the audit committee to establish policies and procedures regarding the receipt, retention, and treatment of complaints regarding violations of accounting and auditing standards, and Section 806 prohibits retaliations against whistle-blowers.[11] Section 806 of the DOF of 2010 provides protections for whistle-blowers in securities fraud cases, and has directed the SEC to establish rules regarding confidential and anonymous submissions of violations of security laws and conduct of fraudulent and unethical activities by public companies.[12] Whistle-blowers are protected and rewarded for informing the SEC of corporate wrongdoings. Whistle-blowers are eligible for awards when:

- information is voluntary (not under subpoena)
- information is original and not public
- information leads to enforcement of action
- whistle-blower complied with procedures
- information is true and correct.

Near and Miceli (1988: 5) define whistle-blowing as the "disclosure by organizational members (former and current) of illegal, immoral, or il-legitimate practices under the control of their employers to persons or organizations that may be able to affect action."[13] Rezaee (2002) states that whistle-blowing implies that an individual with knowledge of wrongdoing informs those with the authority (internal and external to the organization) to remedy the wrong situation.[14] Thus, whistle-blowers are employees or other individuals who decide to challenge their company's abuses of power, violations of any federal criminal fraud against shareholders, or illegality that harm or threaten the public interest. The audit committee play an important role in the design and implementation of the internal whistle-blowing programs as well as reporting of violations of securities laws to the SEC.

Whistle-blowing simply means that an individual with knowledge of wrongdoing decides to reveal that wrongdoing, either through internal channels to individuals (authorities) within the organization, or through external channels to individuals (authorities) outside the organization. Rezaee (2002) describes the internal channel as disclosing wrongdoing to coworkers, management, the audit committee, legal counsel, and/or the board of directors, whereas the external channel can be independent auditors, the media, and/or a governmental agency (e.g., the SEC).[15] Rezaee (2002) discusses a three-step process of whistle-blowing that includes recognition, assessment, and action.[16] In the first step, an individual becomes aware of a wrongdoing. The second step involves the assessment of wrongdoing in terms of whether it deserves action and whether the individual feels responsible for taking the action and disclosing it internally or externally. The third step is that the individual decides whether to remain silent or to report to authorities, and whether to report internally or externally.

Prior to the passage of SOX, whistle-blowers were at high risk of facing harassment, discharge, intimidation, suspension, demotion, dismissal, discrimination, blacklisting, humiliation, and complete destruction of their career and life. Section 806 of the Act provides protection for whistle-blowers by prohibiting a public company from retaliating against whistle-blowers.[17]

The past decade, particularly the post-SOX period, provides a better understanding of what whistle-blowers are and the important role they can play in preventing, reporting, and correcting corporate corruption, fraud, and financial malfeasance. Whistle-blowers at Enron (Sherron Watkins) and WorldCom (Cynthia Cooper) prove that they are often the brightest, best qualified, most courageous, and most committed employees in organizations who risk their employment and life for speaking out about wrongdoings.

Sections 301 and 806 of SOX and SEC-related rules require: (1) the audit committee to establish procedures for the receipt, retention, and treatment of complaints received by the company relevant to accounting, internal accounting control, or auditing matters as well as confidential and anonymous submission by employees of concerns regarding questionable accounting or auditing matters; and (2) that the company provide whistle-blower protections for its employees who willingly report evidence of fraud or violations of securities laws.[18] SOX and the SEC do not require any specific procedures for whistle-blower programs and procedures and give flexibility to the listed companies and their audit committees to establish whistle-blower programs and procedures that are suitable for and tailored to their particular situations.[19]

To facilitate the receipt, retention, and timely responses to complaints and other questionable financial matters, the audit committee should oversee the establishment of whistle-blower programs and procedures. The establishment of whistle-blower programs, policies, and procedures for receiving, investigating, correcting actions, and preventing further violations should go beyond the regulatory requirements of accounting, internal controls, and auditing-related matters, and cover all sorts of complaints including those from customers, suppliers, investors, creditors, employees, and other stakeholders pertaining to product quality, job satisfaction, and environmental matters. These policies and procedures should alert the audit committee of potential concerns before they cause serious consequences.

The regulatory requirements for external whistle-blower programs and the organization's internal programs present audit committees with significant challenges of determining: (1) the individual or department that should be responsible for the success of overall internal and external whistle-blower programs; (2) methods and procedures for the receipt and investigation of both internal and external complaints; (3) communication of investigative results to affected individuals and the proper disclosures if needed; (4) course of action(s) to correct complaints and to prevent their further occurrences; and (5) ways to inform the audit committee regarding the receipt, retention, and treatment of its complaints.

Organizations with effective internal audit functions can use their auditors to assist management under the direct oversight of the audit committee to establish whistle-blower programs, policies, and procedures to receive, investigate, and communicate complaint matters. In the case of the nonexistence of an internal auditing department or in other controversial circumstances, external service providers can be hired to investigate complaint matters under the direct oversight function of the audit committee. In all investigative cases, the audit committee should consult with the organization's legal counsel regarding procedures for receiving and handling complaints.

The Deloitte & Touche 2003 survey indicates that the majority of surveyed public companies have now established and implemented procedures to receive complaints both internally and externally (85 percent and 60 percent, respectively).[20] Companies use both internally operated and third-party administered methods to collect complaints by the means of a telephone hotline, website, and e-mail address. Particularly, a telephone hotline is the most commonly used method to collect complaints according to the survey. The majority of complaints have been received and validated by a general counsel (62 percent), internal auditors (29 percent), and governance/complaint officer (24 percent).[21] The audit committee has received and validated a very small portion of complaints (less than 10 percent), even though the audit committee is in charge of establishing whistle-blower pro-cedures.[22] The majority of received complaints were investigated by general counsel (69 percent) and internal auditors (51 percent), while governance or compliance officers (20 percent) had less involvement in investigations by the audit committee.[23] However, the investigation reports have been provided to the audit committees (60 percent as needed, 18 percent quarterly, and 7 percent annually).[24]

SOX has been criticized for not assigning the investigation of reported complaints and the protection of whistle-blowers to the SEC, the regulatory body charged to investigate violations of securities laws and financial malfeasance.[25] Whistle-blower protection went instead to the Labor Department's Occupational Safety and Health Administration (OSHA) where investigators are trained in health and safety matters and not sophisticated financial shenanigans and fraudulent financial schemes.[26] The effectiveness of OSHA in handling whistle-blower cases for protection under SOX can be very crucial to the long-term success of whistle-blower programs and the willingness of whistle-blowers to speak out about their employers' alleged improprieties. Pursuant to the passage of SOX and until October 2004, OSHA has reviewed 317 complaints by employees reporting mistreatment for raising concerns about alleged fraudulent financial activities by their employers.[27] From this total, 64 were pending, 253 were investigated, and 38 cases resulted in favor of the employee.

Examples of Whistle-blower Programs

A vigorous whistle-blower program can assist in identifying concerns regarding accounting, financial reporting, internal controls, and audit issues, as well as detecting financial statement fraud. The 2004 survey of the Association of Certified Fraud Examiners (ACFE) reveals that the leading method for detecting fraud is through tips received from employees, customers, suppliers, and others, which count for more than 40 percent of the fraud detected.[28] The audit committee should oversee the establishment and operation of an effective whistle-blower program that: (1) promotes a corporate culture that views whistle-blowing as a value-added function of creating an ethical workplace; (2) establishing a confidential reporting mechanism for receiving, retaining, and considering concerns and complaints regarding business, financial accounting, internal controls, and audit issues; and (3) ensures fair treatment of whistle-blowers with no possibility for retribution and retaliation. Exhibit 7.3 presents GM's whistle-blower program including GM AwareLine, grievances, and complaints.

The audit committee should initiate the establishment of a vigorous whistle-blower program and engage internal auditors to operate such a program to ensure direct submission of complaints to the audit committee as well as the assessment of the effectiveness of both the design and operation of the company's whistle-blower program and related procedures including telephone hotlines.

The review of reported financial scandals reveals that often internal personnel voiced concerns, but their allegations did not get reported to the audit committee, or the audit committee did not take proper and timely actions. Thus, the SOX requirements that audit committees be responsible to establish procedures for the receipt, retention, and treatment of accounting and auditing-related complaints should increase the likelihood that improprieties, inappropriate behavior, and fraudulent financial activities will be reported and considered. The audit committee may receive complaints both internally from employees and externally from customers, suppliers, analysts, and the media regarding concerns about business practices and financial reports.

To comply with the whistle-blower provisions of SOX, many companies have established anonymous whistle-blower "hotlines" for employees' confidential submissions of concerns. SOX requires the company's audit committee to establish whistle-blower procedures and oversee their effective operations. Thus, the audit committee should approve, revise, or establish the procedures and policies to address how concerns are raised, retained, reported to the audit committee, and ultimately treated. The audit committee, in effectively overseeing the whistle-blower process, should delegate the responsibility for carrying out the process to the appropriate person such as the compliance officer, the CAE, the ethics officer, the general counsel, or any other key personnel selected by the audit committee. The designated individual should possess objectivity, integrity, maturity, fair judgment, knowledge, skills, ability, and confidence to operate the whistle-blower process (including hotlines under the

Exhibit 7.3

General Motor's whistle-blower program

GM Awareline

Grievances or complaints by employees are handled pursuant to procedures specified in local union labor agreements. Additionally, GM has implemented a 24-hour toll-free telephone reporting system that is available on a global basis seven days per week. The system, GM AwareLine, allows individuals to remain anonymous when reporting concerns, such as:

- Possible criminal wrongdoing by the company, its management, supervisors, employees, or agents
- Actions believed to be contrary to corporate policy (e.g., actions believed to be inconsistent with *General Motors' Guidelines for Employee Conduct*, actions involving substance abuse, etc.)
- Possible emergency, life-threatening situations.

GM business units around the world have customized this reporting process to meet local language and cultural needs. GM operations that choose not to use the *GM AwareLine* process in a given country or location because of legal or cultural reasons must implement an alternate process, which must be approved by GM's General Director of Global Security.

Grievances and complaints

Grievances or complaints by represented employees (generally hourly but may also include non-managerial salaried in some countries) are handled according to the procedures specified in the applicable national and/or local collective bargaining agreements. Procedures for non-represented (typically salaried) employees generally differ from those established for represented employees. For U.S. salaried employees, we manage complaints according to the Open Door Policy, detailed in "Working with GM." This helps ensure open communication with management when employees have a question, concern, or complaint about any aspect of their employment.

Source: Adapted from 2004 Corporate Responsibility Report. Available at: https://awareline. com/SpeakUpPolicy.pdf

oversight function of the audit committee) without any conflict of interest with senior executives.

If the audit committee decides to use the company's hotline as part of the whistle-blower programs, the hotline should be made accessible for 24 hours seven days a week (24/7) and for multinational corporations provide appropriate language and translation capabilities. The hotline can be administered internally or externally. The internally administered hotline must ensure that employee calls are untraceable, confidential, and receive proper consideration. The outsourced hotline provided by external service providers must receive, document calls, and report them to the designated company personnel for further consideration by the audit committee. An externally administered hotline may be perceived by employees and others as more independent and thus may encourage employees to report complaints and concerns. However, security, due diligence, confidentiality, reliability, and availability of a third-party hotline service provider are crucial in ensuring proper receipt, retention, and treatment of complaints.

Complaints received from individuals outside of the company can also be handled internally or externally. The internally administered process for recovering external complaints can be through the hotline to receive external calls, a post office box to facilitate outsiders to write in their concerns, and an e-mail address allowing outsiders to e-mail their complaints. The company should facilitate, encourage, and demonstrate to outside whistle-blowers that their concerns and complaints are taken seriously and investigated properly by promptly acknowledging the receipt of complaints and timely responding to such complaints.

Audit Committee Consideration of Complaints

Companies may receive a large volume of complaints from both internal and external sources that constitutes a serious challenge for them to properly address. Companies should utilize automated tools to track complaints and route them to the designated person. The whistle-blower administrator may receive a variety of complaints related to different issues. The designated hotline of whistle-blower administrators should determine whether complaints relate to human resources, product, safety, and environmental issues or accounting, auditing, and internal control matters. Complaints involving accounting internal controls, financial reporting, and auditing issues that meet certain criteria (materiality threshold, nature, senior management involvement) should be reported to the audit committee for further consideration and investigation, whereas other complaints should be referred to the appropriate department (customer services, human resources, legal, ethics).

The audit committee should establish appropriate policies and procedures for analyzing, investigating, and reporting consequential complaints and overseeing the investigation process. The audit committee should regularly receive a summary report on all consequential complaints pertaining to accounting, audit, internal control, and financial reporting issues as well as material non-financial complaints, their investigations, and resolutions. The audit committee should take proper actions when investigated complaints result in allegations of fraudulent financial activities, violations of applicable laws and regulations, or other material misconduct. The audit committee (and perhaps the entire board of directors) should get involved to manage company reputation issues, damage control, settlement with regulators, handling of lawsuits, enforcement actions by regulators, and final resolution of problems and issues.

The recent corporate governance reforms requiring the establishment of whistle-blower programs by public companies and the roles that whistle-blowers played in bringing Enron and WorldCom to justice have encouraged employees to stand up to company wrongdoing, and to not only refuse to be part of wrongdoing, but also to report their employers for taking part in corporate shenanigans. However, any complaints received by the audit committee should be screened and evaluated on their merits in terms of whether whistle-blowers were sincere in their efforts to: (1) make right a wrong; (2) protect themselves from being implicated; and (3) take revenge for seemingly unjustifiable and undesirable treatment.

The audit committee should assure confidentiality of whistle-blowers and protect their rights, interests, and employment for the possibility of being fired immediately or any future retaliation. Whistle-blowers should receive fair treatment and not be viewed as outcasts who betray their employers. The audit committee should also consider that employees' participation in the company's ownership through stock options and stock in retirement funds makes it more difficult for employees to speak out (or at least makes them think twice) about whether their whistle-blowing actions could result in a substantial drop in their investment value (stock prices). Perhaps employees' financial ties to the company and the culture of employees being viewed as part of the corporate family are the primary reasons for employees not to come forward to report their company's wrongdoings (e.g., Enron).

The audit committee should establish toll-free hotlines or even an ombudsperson or an inspector general's office to: (1) facilitate employees voicing their concerns; (2) ensure anonymity of their complaints; (3) guarantee consideration of their reported wrongdoings with no possible retaliation against them; (4) investigate reported complaints and concerns with respect, integrity, and fairness; and (5) maintain strict confidentiality about receiving complaints, treatment of complaints, and actions taken.[29]

There is an increased awareness on the part of employees that SOX provides protection to them for reporting wrongdoings, and thus whistle-blowing activities have substantially increased in the past several years. Public companies' boards of directors have received steadily increasing reports of their company's internal allegations of accounting, auditing, and internal control concerns, and the SEC received more than 180,000 complaints in 2003 and 250,000 complaints in 2004 for possible violations of securities laws.[30]

Audit Committee Whistle-blower Procedures

Part II (C) of the SEC final rule[31] deals with complaint procedures that audit committees must adopt. Under the listing standards called for by the final rules, each audit committee must establish procedures for:

1. The receipt, retention, and treatment of complaints received by the issuer regarding accounting, internal accounting controls, or auditing matters, and
2. The confidential, anonymous submission by employees of the issuer of concerns regarding questionable accounting or auditing matters.

Other than those two guidelines, the rules leave audit committees free to institute whistle-blower programs as they see fit based on their company-specific needs. The audit committee is responsible for setting up the reporting mechanism. It cannot rely on management to develop procedures, because "the very purpose of the system is to create an information system that bypasses management."[32]

Section 301 of SOX regarding whistle-blower mechanisms for the receipt, retention, and treatment of complaints covers only internal and external accounting, auditing, and internal control matters. SOX does not address general complaints regarding customer or supplier dissatisfaction and employment-related issues. Nevertheless, it is appropriate that the audit committee, in establishing whistle-blower programs to meet the mandatory regulatory requirements, also consider and incorporate general complaints in addition to auditing, accounting, and internal control complaints. The audit committee should oversee the company's whistle-blower program procedures and complaint mechanisms, which are designed for concerned individuals to report wrongdoings to authorities or persons in a position to prevent and correct wrongdoings.

Retaliation and Whistle-blowing

In the year 2002, three women (Cynthia Cooper, an internal auditor with the bankrupted WorldCom; Colleen Rowley, an agent with the U.S. Federal Bureau of Investigation; and Sherron Watkins, an executive of Enron) were named as Time Magazine's 2002 "Persons of the Year."[33] These women were courageous and felt an ethical obligation to blow the whistle when their employer was engaged in unethical and inappropriate activities. Cynthia Cooper, in performing an internal audit in May 2002, detected irregularities in the accounting practices of WorldCom related to the recognition of expenses. She discovered that WorldCom had been recognizing operating costs as capital expenditures to inflate its earnings. She communicated her audit findings to the audit committee and further investigation revealed that the company overstated its earnings by $11 billion, which resulted in the largest corporate bankruptcy in U.S. history. SOX requires whistle-blowers to report their complaints and concerns to the audit committee.

In 2002, the National Whistleblower Center (NWC) conducted a survey of whistle-blowers from 200 cases reported to the NWC, in which 59.5 percent of the respondents were male and 40.5 percent were female.[34] A little over half (51 percent) blew the whistle on fraud or criminal practices. The report suggests that retaliation against whistle-blowers is still common. About 50 percent (99 respondents) alleged that they were terminated after they blew the whistle, whereas the other 101 respondents acknowledged on-the-job harassment or discipline.[35] U.S. companies are facing an increase in employment-related retaliation claims. "According to the U.S. Equal Employment Opportunity Commission (EEOC), the number of retaliation charges more than doubled to 22,768 from 11,096 between 1992 and 2002.[36] These claims accounted for 27 percent of all EEOC claims in 2002, compared with 15.3 percent in 1992."[37] The audit committee should ensure that whistle-blowers are protected and are not unjustifiably retaliated against for coming forward to report the company's wrongdoings, particularly financial malfeasance.

Whistle-Blowing Program

Whistle-blowing is defined as "the disclosure by organization members (former or current) of illegal, immoral, or illegitimate practices under the control of their employers, to persons or organizations that may be able to effect action."[38] Whistle-blowing programs should be established and monitored because the consequences of whistle-blowing are significant and can range from personal retaliation such as termination to organizational risks such as continuation of wrongdoing or controversy over policy changes. Anonymously blowing the whistle may offer some protection to the whistle-blower, but the effectiveness of an investigation may be reduced. Public companies are required to establish and enforce a whistle-blower program under the SOX of 2002, and DOF of 2010, private companies, and nonprofit organizations, although not required by law, can benefit from the best practices of whistle-blowing. The audit committee is typically responsible for overseeing the establishment and enforcement of whistle-blower programs in compliance with the requirements of SOX, DOF, and SEC, and other related rules and regulations.

SOX initially created the opportunity for confidential and anonymous submissions of complaints by requiring that the company's audit committee establish procedures for the collection and treatment of such complaints. The DOF of 2010 underscored the importance of effective whistle-blowing program in protecting consumers and investors from corporate wrongdoings. DOF is also intended to improve the effectiveness of corporate whistle-blowing programs by providing protection for whistle-blowers and offering rewards for the risk they take. It provides significant new incentives for employees and others to blow the whistle when they become aware of violations of laws and fraud within a company. Under Section 922 of the act, a person who provides "original information" about a securities law violation to the SEC, which then leads to a successful enforcement action with penalties of $1 million or more, is now entitled to collect 10 to 30 percent of the total penalties imposed by the agency.

In August 2011, the Commodity Futures Trading Commission (CFTC) adopted final regulations implementing the whistle-blower provision for the DOF of 2010 (Section 748).[39] The adopted CFTC's whistle-blower requires the CFTC to pay a reward to whistle-blowers who provide information relevant to the assessment of monetary sanctions against those who violated the Commodity Exchange Act (CEA). This regulation is broad enough that can be applied by any employee or nonemployee who presents information regarding any possible violation of the CEA. Dodd–Frank Section 748 also establishes effective anti-retaliation protections for whistle-blowers. The CFTC's regulation is consistent with SEC' final rules on whistle-blower program.

Individuals become eligible for whistle-blowing awards under SEC regulations of both the CFTC and SEC when:

1. The information provided is considered as voluntary. The voluntary information must be submitted before the individual under subpoena or otherwise is required to present the information (inquiries or demands by Congress, Courts, Department of Justice, State and Federal Authorities, Self-regulatory Organizations). Normally, information is not considered voluntary if the individual is required to submit the information under a preexisting legal or contractual

obligation to the regulatory or law enforcement authorities or the designated agency.

2. The whistle-blower's submission is considered as original information not available from public sources (e.g., fillings with the SEC, the media) and is derived from the whistle-blower's independent knowledge or independent analysis based on public information not available elsewhere.

3. The whistle-blower's submission must lead to successful enforcement of an administrative or a judicial action against the wrongdoer.

4. The whistle-blower has fully complied with stated procedures for providing the valuable information (submission online, e-mail, mail, and fax).

5. The submitted information is true and correct to the best of the whistle-blower's knowledge and belief.

The DOF and SEC and CFTC-related regulations provide whistle-blowers with two primary types of protections. First, the whistle-blower's identity is typically kept confidential unless and until the identity is required to be disclosed to a defendant or respondent in a government proceeding. Second, whistle-blowers are normally allowed to bring a private cause of action against their employers for retaliation against their actions. According to the SEC rule on whistle-blowing, a whistle-blower can receive a bounty of up to 30% of the government's recovery when cases involved are in excess of $1 million. Public companies should: (1) establish an effective internal whistle-blowing reporting program that enables employees to internally report corporate wrongdoings, (2) create the right tone at the top providing incentives and mechanism for whistle-blowers to come forward, (3) communicate with employees about the internal reporting mechanisms and how they interact with the SEC's whistle-blower rules, and (4) educate managers about the anti-retaliation provisions of the SEC's whistle-blower rules to prevent inappropriate retaliatory employment actions against employees who either come forward internally or go directly to the SEC.

The Dodd-Frank Wall Street Reform and Consumer Protection Act authorized the SEC to pay financial rewards to whistle-blowers who provide credible new and timely information about any securities law violation. The SEC established the office of whistle-blowing program and the new webpage at www.sec.gov/whistleblower, which provide information on eligibility requirements, instruction for submitting a tip or complaint and applying for an award including answers to frequently asked questions. The SEC WB program is intended to strengthen the SEC's role of protecting investors in the following ways:[40]

- **Better Tips**: The WB program has increased the quality and quantity of tips received by the SEC on violations of security laws.
- **Timely Tips**: Potential whistle-blowers are incentivized to come forward with "timely" and credible information not yet known to the SEC.
- **Maximizes Outside Resources**: The program assists the SEC to more effectively and efficiently utilize its resources to discover violations of the security laws.
- **New Protections against Retaliation**: Employees who come forward are better protected against potential retaliatory actions by employers.
- **Bolsters Internal Compliance**: The SEC WB program encourages employees to report any wrongdoing to their company's internal compliance department reporting to the SEC.

The SEC released its whistle-blowing rule in May 2011, which provides a monetary incentive of between 10 and 30 percent to a successful SEC action, with sanctions exceeding $1 million for WB who voluntarily provide the SEC with original information that leads the sanction. Several important issues about the SEC final rules on WB program are[41]:

1. The SEC final rule on whistle-blower program is intended to bolster, not hamper, the company's internal compliance systems at companies across the country—the rules specify that employees may benefit in two significant ways when they report wrongdoing internally first and, within 120 days report it to the SEC.

2. Attorneys, compliance personnel, and external auditors are not allowed to become whistle-blowers except under the specific circumstances permitted in the final rules.

3. The whistle-blower program ensures that efforts to address misconduct are sped up, not delayed. Employees are not allowed to delay reporting ongoing misconduct to increase the size of the sanctions and thus their potential award.

Conclusion

The ever-increasing laws, rules, regulations, and standards demand that public companies establish a compliance and ethics officer position that operates under the audit committee oversight function. Both SOX Act of 2002 and DOF Act of 2010 and SEC-related implementation rules enable the audit committee to establish proper whistle-blowing policies and procedures to encourage employees come forward and inform the audit committee of severe violations of securities laws and fraud as well as unethical behavior. The audit committee should conduct an internal investigation and protect whistle-blowers from any retaliations. The audit committee is responsible for ensuring that the company is conducting its business ethically and is in compliance with all legal and regulatory requirements. The audit committee should review and approve the company's code of business conduct and compliance process and ensure compliance with both the code and compliance programs.

Action Items

1. Review the system of compliance with legal and regulatory requirements.

2. Ensure the code of business conduct is established, communicated with employees, enforced, and periodically reviewed and updated.

3. Ensure the establishment of the chief compliance and ethics executive position that directly reports to the audit committee.

4. Establish effective internal whistle-blowing program.

5. Create tone at the top to encourage whistle-blowers to come forward.

6. Communicate with employees the whistle-blowing program.

7. Educate managers about anti-retaliation provision of the established whistle-blowing program.
8. Established codes of ethics and ethics programs address the following:
   • Avoidance and resolution of conflicts
   • Compliance with all applicable regulations
   • Emphasis on customer relations
   • Avoidance of improper use of confidential information
   • Encouragement of whistle-blowers

Endnotes

1. Rezaee, Z. 2007. Corporate Governance Post-Sarbanes-Oxley. Regulations, Requirements, and Integrated Processes. New Jersey: John Wiley & Son
2. SOX. 2002. Section 406.
3. Securities and Exchange Commission (SEC). 2003. Disclosure Required by Section 406 and 407 of the Sarbanes-Oxley Act of 2002 (January 23). Release No. 338177. Available at: www.sec.gov/rules/final/33-8177a.htm
4. The Committee of Sponsoring Organizations of the Treadway Commission (COSO). 1987. *Report of the National Commission on Fraudulent Financial Reporting.* Washington, DC: U.S. Government Office.
5. Ibid.
6. New York Stock Exchange (NYSE). 2004. Final NYSE Corporate Governance Rules. Available at: www.ecgi.org/codes/documents/finalcorpgovrules.pdf
7. Rezaee, Z., & Lander, G. H. 1993. The Internal Auditor's Relationship with the Audit Committee. *Managerial Auditing Journal* 8(3): 35–40.
8. Dallas/IABC. Survey of Executive Integrity (January). Available at: www.dallasiabc.com
9. Sarbanes-Oxley Act. 2002. Section 301. Available at: www.sec.gov/about/laws/soa2002.pdf
10. SOX Section 301. SEC. 2003. Standards relating to listed company audit committees (April 9). Rule No. 33-8220). Available at: www.sec.gov/rules/final/33-8220.htm
11. SOX 2002. Section 406.

12. Dodd–Frank Act of 2010.

13. Near, J., & Miceli, M. 1988. *The Internal Auditor's Ultimate Responsibility: The Reporting of Sensitive Issues.* Altamonte Springs, FL: Institute of Internal Auditors.

14. Rezaee, Z. 2002. *Financial Statement Fraud: Prevention and Detection.* New York, NY: John Wiley & Sons.

15. Ibid.

16. Ibid.

17. SOX. 2002. Section 806 SEC. 2003 (April 9).

18. Sarbanes-Oxley Act, 2002. Securities and Exchange Commission (SEC). 2003. SEC Final Rule: Standards Relating To Listed Company Audit Committees. Release Nos. 33-8220; 34-47654. (April 9). Available at: www.sec.gov/rules/final/33-8220.htm.

19. SEC. 2003. Standards Relating To Listed Company Audit Committees. Release Nos. 33-8220; 34-47654 (April 9). Available at: www.sec.gov/rules/final/33-8220.htm

20. Deloitte & Touche. 2003. Audit committee Financial Expert Designation and Disclosure Practice Survey. Available at: www.deloitte.com/dtt/article/0,1002,sid%253D2006%2526cid%253D13514,00.html

21. Ibid.

22. Ibid.

23. Ibid.

24. Ibid.

25. Solomon, D. 2004. For Financial Whistle-Blowers, New Shield Is an Imperfect One. *The Wall Street Journal* A1.

26. Ibid.

27. Ibid.

28. Association of Certified Fraud Examiners (ACFE). 2004. *Report to the Nation on Occupational Fraud and Abuse.* Austin, TX: ACFE: 18.

29. For more in depth information about ombudsperson job descriptions, standards of ethics, and standards of practices, visit the Web site of the Ombudsman Association at www.ombuds-toa.org/

30. Farrel, G. 2004. Accounting Leads Rise, Making Boards Edgy. *USA Today* (July 30). Available at: http://usatoday30.usatoday.com/money/companies/management/2004-07-29-whistle-side-1b_x.htm

31. SEC. 2003.

32. *Anonymous*. 2004. Pass the Aspirin. *American Banking Association Banking Journal* 96(2): 26–28.

33. Lacayo, R., & Ripley, A. 2002. Time 2002 Persons of the Year: Cynthia Cooper, Coleen Rowley, and Sherron Watkins. *Time* (December 12). Available at: www.time.com/time/personoftheyear/2002/

34. National Whistleblower Center. 2002. Labor Day Report: the National Status of Whistleblower Protection on Labor Day, 2002. Available at: www.gpo.gov/fdsys/pkg/CRI-2002/html/CRI-2002-NATIONAL-WHISTLEBLOWER-CENTER.htm

35. Ibid.

36. Judy Greenwald. 2004. Retaliation Claims a Growing Concern. *Business Insurance* 38(1): 4–6.

37. Ibid.

38. Near, J. P., & Miceli, M. P. 1985. Organizational Dissidence: The Case of Whistleblowing. *Journal of Business Ethics* 4(1):1–16.

39. The U.S Commodity Futures Trading Commission (CFTC). 2011. Whistleblower Incentives and Protection. Final Rule, Federal Register/Vol 76, No.165. Available at: http://cftc.gov/ucm/groups/public/@lrfederalregister/documents/file/2011-20423a.pdf

40. U.S. Securities and Exchange Commission. 2011. SEC's New Whistleblower Program Takes Effect Today. Washington, D.C. (August 12, 2011). Available at: www.sec.gov/news/press/2011/2011-167.htm

41. U.S. Securities and Exchange Commission. 2011. Speech by SEC Staff: Remarks at Georgetown University, Sean X. McKessy, Chief, Office of the Whistleblower Washington, D.C. (August 11, 2011). Available at: www.sec.gov/news/speech/2011/spch081111sxm.htm

CHAPTER 8

Tax Oversight Function of the Audit Committee

Executive Summary

Business transactions and financial reporting are impacted by taxes in several ways including sales tax, value-added tax, customs, duties, intercompany taxes, and income taxes. Corporate income taxes, proper compliance with tax rules and regulations, and tax planning require considerable judgments and estimates by the management. These judgments and estimates can have a significant impact on the accuracy and fairness of financial reports. Management judgments, policies, and practices for all types of corporate taxes should be reviewed and approved by the audit committee. This chapter discusses the audit committee oversight function over tax considerations.

Introduction

The entire tax system in the United States is based on self-reporting and compliance and as such while some forms of income tax reporting involve information easily verifiable (W2 income) by the Internal Revenue Service (IRS), a significant amount of tax information is almost unverifiable (undocumented cash-based income). Furthermore, management uses its judgments in determining corporate taxes through tax planning and tax avoidance schemes. The fact that the IRS relies heavily on unverifiable tax information has resulted in significant noncompliance (approximately $450 billion)[1]. Since the passage of SOX, many provisions of income tax services have received significant amounts of attention from lawmakers, regulators, and standard-setters. For example, Securities and Exchange Commission (SEC) Chief Accountant Donald Nicolaisen, in his remarks at the Tax Council Institute Conference in February 2004, stated, "The accounting and reporting of income taxes has received increased scrutiny by investigators, analysts, Congress, and others. Accurately accounting for the income tax consequences of a company's transaction is critical to the credibility of the financial statements as a whole."[2]

Audit Committees and Taxes

Corporate taxes can affect both the operational results and financial position of public companies as indicated in the KPMG reports and presented in Exhibit 8.1.[3] The audit committee should oversee tax risk assessment, tax planning, tax compliance, tax accounting and reporting, and management of tax estimates and judgments to ensure the reliability, integrity, and quality of financial reports. Audit committees are not expected to be experts in tax risk assessment. Indeed, the majority (56 percent) of the participants of KPMG's 2003 roundtable indicate that improvement is needed in the process utilized by their audit committee to oversee effectively the financial reporting implications of taxes.[4] Nevertheless, audit committees should consider taxes as part of their oversight function and ask management relevant questions pertaining to tax risk assessment, tax planning, tax compliance, tax accounting, and reporting. KPMG suggests the following fundamental elements of the tax oversight function of the audit committee:[5]

1. The competence of tax personnel, both internal and external, in carrying out their tax-assigned responsibilities.
2. Managerial policies and procedures designed to ensure compliance with the company's applicable tax laws and regulations.
3. The adequacy and effectiveness of internal controls over tax accounting and reporting.
4. The legitimacy and reasonableness of managerial judgments and estimates involving tax compliance and reporting.
5. The appropriateness of accounting for, and the effects of taxes on, financial reports and their proper disclosures.
6. The extent and significance of the company's tax exposure items, tax contingencies, tax-advantaged transactions, and tax uncertainties.

Exhibit 8.1

Tax is embedded in every aspect of business

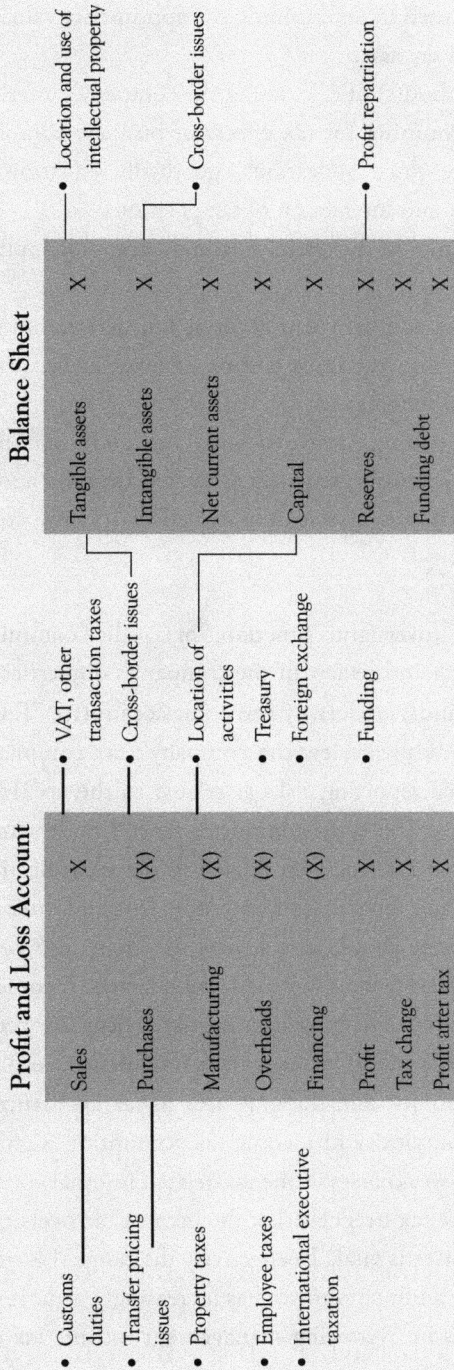

Profit and Loss Account

Sales	X
Purchases	(X)
Manufacturing	(X)
Overheads	(X)
Financing	(X)
Profit	X
Tax charge	X
Profit after tax	X

- Customs duties
- Transfer pricing issues
- Property taxes
- Employee taxes
- International executive taxation

- VAT, other transaction taxes
- Cross-border issues
- Location of activities
- Treasury
- Foreign exchange
- Funding

Balance Sheet

Tangible assets	X
Intangible assets	X
Net current assets	X
Capital	X
Reserves	X
Funding debt	X

- Location and use of intellectual property
- Cross-border issues
- Profit repatriation

Source: Adapted from KPMG. 2003. Tax Risk and Responsibility Publication: Identifying and Managing Risk in the Post-Sarbanes-Oxley Act Business Environment. Available at: http://kpmg.com/aci/

7. Factors used in determining the appropriate valuation allowance for deferred tax assets.
8. The method(s) of calculating the company's interim taxes.
9. The accounting for tax effects of business combinations including purchase price allocations, goodwill, valuation allowance, stock options, and interaction of tax positions.
10. Monitoring of the effective compliance with applicable tax laws and regulations.
11. Ways the company can account for, determines the effects of, and discloses income taxes and other taxes in its quarterly and annual financial statements.
12. Proper communications with the audit committee and major stakeholders on tax issues to ensure that the audit committee understands and assesses the tax effects on the company's financial reports.

The tax oversight function of audit committee requires an understanding and review of the company's domestics and international tax policies and practices by the audit committee. The audit committee should periodically review the company's tax compliance risks and relevant financial reporting risks as related to the tax shifting and transfer pricing abuses. The audit committee should understand and review risk assessment and management related to the identification, measurement, recognition, and reporting of both domestic and international taxes. The audit committee should also review the company's compliance with all applicable domestic and international tax laws. Income tax accounting is one of the most challenging areas primarily because of continuous changes in tax laws, the use of management judgment in estimating taxable income and liability, and the gray area of tax avoidance and tax evasion. Given the complexity of income tax accounting, significant deficiencies and material weaknesses in the tax-related internal controls and possibilities of income tax irregularities, the income tax oversight function of the audit committee is vital. To effectively discharge this important oversight function, the audit committee has increasingly dedicated substantial time and resources in overseeing management income tax consideration and accounting.

The audit committee is authorized to hire advisers and outside service providers to assist the audit committee in overseeing the following:[6]

1. Management strategies and activities in coordinating and sharing of tax information between multiple corporate departments and geographies including accounting, finance, operations, treasury, tax, and human resources.
2. Management judgment and estimates in the complexity and highly judgment-based nature of the income tax accounting laws and standard.
3. Management discretions in addressing the challenges associated with the ever-changing tax laws of extraordinary detail and complexity in multiple jurisdictions.

The audit committees should ask the following income tax questions from management, accountants, and auditors[7]:

1. Is income tax accounting in compliance with all applicable tax laws and accounting standards?
2. What are the key tax assumptions and estimates supporting financial statement estimates and assertions as well as disclosures?
3. How does management ensure timely cross-functional coordination between all affected departments and geographic jurisdictions?
4. Is there a basic understanding of key tax high-stakes issues and estimates between management and auditors?
5. What internal controls are designed and implemented to ensure reliable financial reporting and compliance with tax laws and tax accounting standards?
6. Are the fees paid to the auditors for tax services properly disclosed?

Corporate Income Taxes

The company's CEO must sign the corporate federal income tax return as required by the Section 1001 of Sarbanes–Oxley Act (SOX).[8] These requirements direct more management attention to tax issues and more vigorous internal control activities and procedures related to tax function. Greater management scrutiny of tax issues and related internal controls should assist companies to better measure their corporate income taxes and their impact on financial statement disclosures. Thus, audit committees should review their company's appropriateness of tax provision, financial statement tax disclosures, and compliance with relevant tax laws, rules, and requirements.

The audit committee should pay particular attention to the company's corporate income taxes for several reasons. First, the company's CEO is now required to sign the corporate income tax return, which warrants more scrutiny by regulators and tax legislators and the investing public. Second, the numerous corporate taxes affect almost every aspect of the company's business and its financial statement disclosures as shown in Exhibit 9.1 adapted from KPMG's Tax Risk and Responsibility Publication.[9] Third, the proposed auditing standards that the Public Company Accounting Oversight Board (PCAOB) has submitted to the SEC for approval would prohibit the independent auditor from performing a variety of tax services simultaneously with auditing a public company.[10] Fourth, tax risks are associated with both external sources due to complexity and ever-changing tax laws, rules, and regulations as well as internal corporate events, transactions, and operations (e.g., mergers and acquisitions, oversees operations). Finally, PCAOB Auditing Standards No. 2 pertaining to internal controls addresses tax compliance and reporting function as part of tests of controls on the company's control activities.[11] While management is responsible for establishing adequate and effective internal controls over tax-related activities, the independent auditor should assess the effectiveness of these controls.

Management should identify tax risks associated with both internal and external sources, design proper controls to mitigate such risks, and properly document tax control procedures as part of its assessment of internal control over financial reporting. A lack of proper documentation of tax controls and compliance prevents management from assessing the effectiveness of internal control over financial reporting. A lack of a proper tax process, procedures, and controls may also be viewed by the independent auditor as a significant deficiency or an indicator of material weakness in internal control over financial reporting. For the above mentioned reasons, the audit committee should review the company's: (1) tax policies, processes, and procedures for tax activities, operations, planning, and filings; (2) tax risks arising from both internal and external sources; (3) tax controls designed to address tax risks; (4) tax documentation and retention requirements; (5) permissible tax services approved and provided by the independent auditor.

SOX permits auditors to provide non-audit activities "including tax services" that are not specifically prohibited. The SEC final rules specifically include "tax compliance, tax planning, and tax advice" in those non-audit tax services that are allowable.[12]

The SEC Rule defines these tax terms:[13]

Tax compliance generally involves preparation of original and amended tax returns, claims for refund and tax payment–planning services. Tax planning and tax advice encompass a diverse range of services, including assistance with tax audits and appeals, tax advice related to mergers and acquisitions, employee benefit plans, and requests for rulings or technical advice from taxing authorities.

The SEC final rules state that any non-audit tax service that would "impair the independence of the accountant" is prohibited. In the proposed rules, the SEC offered three principles to determine auditor independence in regard to non-audit services: (1) an auditor cannot function in the role of management; (2) an auditor cannot audit his or her own work; and (3) an auditor cannot serve in an advocacy role for his or her client. The final rules, however, abandoned this three-pronged approach in favor of a more subjective approach, because evaluating the provision of tax services with the three basic principles would exclude many tax services historically provided by the independent auditor. The burden of deciding whether a non-audit tax service is prohibited or allowable falls on the audit committee. The only guidance to audit committees and auditors for the determination of the prohibition of the non-audit tax service is given in Footnote 111 of the Final Rules: "It would not be appropriate to provide a prohibited service, label it a 'tax service,' and argue that it is, therefore, permissible."[14] The intention of this footnote is to prevent other non-audit services from being labeled tax services so that auditing firms might provide them to audit clients. However, the footnote also stresses the fact that not all non-audit tax services are permissible without question.

Disclosure of Tax Fees

The SEC Final Rule, Strengthening the Commission's Requirements Regarding Auditor Independence, requires the disclosure of fees paid to the auditing firm in each of the two most recent fiscal years for both its audit and non-audit services. The SEC Rule divides these professional fees into four categories: (1) Audit Fees; (2) Audit-Related Fees; (3) Tax Fees; and (4) All Other Fees.[15] All tax services related to the audit "to the extent that such services are necessary to comply with GAAS" would be included in the audit fee category.[16] Thus, all fees from non-audit tax services would be incorporated in the tax fees category. The company must disclose the nature of the tax services provided in the subcategories of tax compliance, planning, and advisory services, but need not break the tax fees down between these categories.

PCAOB *Proposal Related to Taxes*

In December 2004, the PCAOB issued ethics and independence rules concerning independence, tax services, and contingent fees.[17] The proposed rule would prohibit two types of contingent tax planning and aggressive tax shelters of non-audit tax services. However, the proposed rule specifically identifies other types of tax services that would be permissible as non-audit tax services: (1) routine tax return and tax compliance; (2) general tax planning and advice; (3) international assignment tax services; and (4) employee personal tax services. Under general tax planning and advice, the board distinguishes between "routine" tax planning services initiated by the audit client and "aggressive strategies" marketed by the public accounting firm. These aggressive strategies create a "mutuality of interest."

The IRS has created a list of transactions that have a high risk of being disallowed by the IRS due to a less conservative interpretation of the tax code. Code Sec. 6011 and Code Sec. 6111 require disclosure of possible corporate tax shelter/tax avoidance activity. The IRS has updated descriptions of various transactions previously issued in 2003 and identified them as "listed transactions."[18] New tax legislation, The American Jobs Creation Act of 2004, was enacted on October 22, 2004 to improve U.S. companies' global competitiveness.[19] Section 815 of the Act amended § 6111 to require certain disclosures from tax advisors regarding any reportable transaction: (1) information identifying and describing the transaction and (2) information describing any potential tax benefits expected to result from the transaction.[20]

The PCAOB's proposed standard would prohibit the independent auditor from providing tax treatments that match or are similar to any "listed transactions." Any such tax planning that appears on the list "at the time it is executed" would per se be a prohibited non-audit tax service. The previously executed transaction later becoming a transaction listed by the IRS could imply auditor independence impairment. Any tax planning paired with tax-advisor-imposed confidentiality would also constitute a per se prohibited non-audit tax service under PCAOB's proposed standard, as such confidentiality usually implies a potentially unreliable tax product. In addition, any tax planning based on an aggressive tax position would also be a per se prohibited non-audit tax service.

Although the public accounting firm may provide employees of the auditing client with personal tax services as a non-audit tax service, under the PCAOB proposed standards, tax services for senior officers of the audit client would be per se prohibited non-audit tax services. The independent auditor must still seek pre-approval from the audit committee to provide other employees with personal tax services but are now prohibited from providing personal tax services to specific audit client officers whether paid by the audit client or the executive.

The PCAOB Proposed standard places more responsibility on the public accounting firm to communicate certain items to the audit committee during the pre-approval process, including:[21]

1. Providing the audit committee detailed documentation of the nature and scope of the proposed tax service;
2. Discussing with the audit committee the potential effects on the firm's independence that could be caused by the firm's performance of the proposed tax service; and
3. Documenting the firm's discussion with the audit committee.

The proposed PCAOB standard does not provide audit committees any guidance on how to determine whether a non-audit tax service is permissible or prohibited. The audit committee must use the information provided by the public accounting firm to decide what is best for its shareholders. The proposed rule also addresses contingent fees and makes clear that the auditing firm cannot base fees for non-audit tax services on tax savings it provided to its clients.

The PCAOB proposal identifies four circumstances that would be considered as impairing an auditor's independence. These circumstances are when auditors are: (1) entering into contingent fee arrangements with their clients for performing tax services and charging based on the percentage of tax saving for their client; (2) performing tax services pertaining to tax plans or opinions on tax consequences of a transactions that Treasury Department has specified as a listed or confidential transaction; (3) providing "aggressive tax planning"; or (4) providing tax services to officers in a financial reporting oversight role of their clients.[22]

Aggressive tax planning is defined as any tax planning or opinion that meet all of the following criteria: (1) the auditor provides any service pertaining to the tax plan or opinion; (2) the idea was not initiated by the client; (3) a significant purpose of the idea was to avoid taxes; and (4) the tax plan has a less than 50–50 chance of prevailing if challenged by the Internal Revenue Service.[23] Under the PCAOB auditing proposal, tax services that would be allowed include: (1) routine and usual tax return preparation and tax compliance; (2) general tax planning and advice; (3) employee personal tax services; and (4) international assignment tax services.[24] These permissible tax services should be pre-approved by the company's audit committee to be performed by the independent auditor.

On July 24, 2007, the PCAOB proposed its new *Ethics and Independence Rule 3526* concerning communications with audit committees and an amendment to its existing tax services rule along with an implementation schedule for the tax services rule.[25] The proposed rule 3526 would require independent auditors to communicate to the company's audit committee any relationships between the audit firms and the company that may reasonably be thought to bear on auditor independence. This communication would be required both before the auditor accepts a new engagement and annually for continuing engagements. Although SOX and SEC-related implementation rules permit certain tax services to be performed by the company's independent auditor contemporaneously with audit services, the PCAOB in its *Ethics and Independence Rule 3523* limits the performance of a number of tax services such as tax shelters.

Conclusion

The entire tax system in the United States is based on self-reporting and compliance and management uses its discretion and judgments in determining the timing and amount of corporate taxes. Taxes affect the entire financial reporting process from identification of business wrongdoings to measurement, recognition, and final preparation of financial statements. The audit committee should oversee the company's tax risk assessment, tax planning, tax accounting, tax compliance, and tax reporting to ensure reliability, integrity, quality, and transparency of financial reports. The audit committee should communicate with the company's independent auditor about the company's critical tax accounting policies, tax estimates, and tax planning.

Action Items

1. Ensure the company's tax fairness, transparency, and morality.
2. Ensure compliance with all applicable domestic and international tax laws.
3. Review the processes used by management in identifying, measuring, recognizing, and reporting all corporate tax provisions.
4. Review and approve risk assessment and management of uncertain tax positions, significant tax judgments and estimates, transfer pricing schemes, and taxation of major transactions.
5. Prevent the perceived transfer pricing abuses relevant to the profit shifting and related taxes.
6. Understand and review the company's domestic and international tax provisions and related financial and compliance risks.

Endnotes

1. The estimated tax gap per the IRS was $385 billion in 2006 even after enforcement actions were undertaken to close it from the original $450 billion. Available at: www.irs.gov/uac/IRS-Releases-New-Tax-Gap-Estimates;-Compliance-Rates-Remain-Statistically-Unchanged-From-Previous-Study

2. Nicolaisen, D. 2004. Remarks of the SEC's Chief Accountant at the Tax Council Institute Conference on the Corporate Tax Practice: Responding to the New Challenges of a Changing Landscape. (February). Available at: www.sec.gov/news/speech/spch021104dtn.htm

3. KPMG. 2003. Tax Risk and Responsibility: Identifying and Managing Risk in the Post-Sarbanes-Oxley Business Environment. Available at: www.kpmg.com/aci/

4. Ibid.

5. KPMG. 2003. Audit Committee Oversight of Taxes and Other Issues. Audit Committee Institute (Fall). Available at: www.kpmg.com/aci.

6. PricewaterhouseCoopers (PwC). 2012. Board Room Direct. Income Tax Accounting-Do you Understand It? November 2012. Available at: www.pwc.com/us/en/corporate-governance/publications/directors-and-it.html

7. Ibid.

8. Section 1001 of SOX specifically states that "it is the sense of the Senate that the Federal income tax return of a corporation should be signed by the chief executive officer of such corporation."

9. KPMG. 2003

10. PCAOB. Release No. 2004-015: Proposed Ethics and Independence Rules Concerning Independence, Tax Services and Contingent Fees. (December 14, 2014). Available at: www.pcaobus.org/Rules_of_the_Board/Documents/Docket_017 IRelease20-04-015.pdf.

11. Public Company Accounting Oversight Board (PCAOB). 2004. Auditing Standard No. 2: An Audit of Internal Control over Financial Reporting Performed in Conjunction with an Audit of Financial Statements. Available at: http://pcaobus.org/Rules_of_the_Board/Documents/Rules_of_the_Board/Auditing_Standard_2.pdf

12. SEC. 2003. Release No. 33-8183.

13. Ibid.

14. SEC Release No. 33-8183.

15. Ibid.

16. Ibid.

17. PCAOB. Release No. 2004-015.

18. IRS Notice 2004-80, 2004-50 IRB (November 16, 2004). Available at: www.irs.gov/pub/irs-irbs/irb04-50.pdf

19. The American Jobs Creation Act of 2004. P.L. 108-357, 118 stat. 1418. Available at: www.irs.gov/irb/2004-50_IRB/ar09.html#d0e354

20. IRS Notice 2004-80, 2004-50 IRB (November 16, 2004). Available at: www.pcaobus.org/Rules_of_the_Board/Documents/ Docket_017 IRelease20-04-015.pdf.

21. Ibid.

22. Public Company Accounting Oversight Board. 2004. Release No. 2004-015: Proposed Ethics and Independence Rules Concerning Independence, Tax Services, and Contingent Fees. Available at: www.pcaobus.org/Rules_of_the_Board/Documents/Docket_017/ Release2004-015.pdf

23. Ibid.

24. Ibid.

25. Public Company Accounting Oversight Board (PCAOB). 2007. Board Proposes New Ethics and Independence Rule Concerning Communications with Audit Committees and an Amendment to Its Existing Tax Services Rule and Adjusts Implementation Schedule for Tax Services Rule (July 24). Available at: www.pcaob.org/ News_and_Events/News/2007/07-24.aspx.

Index

www.ingramcontent.com/pod-product-compliance
Lightning Source LLC
Chambersburg PA
CBHW060547210326
41519CB00014B/3387